Sinister Wisdom 126
Fall 2022

Publisher: Sinister Wisdom, Inc.
Editor & Publisher: Julie R. Enszer
Associate Editor: Sierra Earle
Guest Editors: Jane Segal and Brooke Lober
The guest editors extend special thanks to: Jennifer Beach, Claude Marks, Freedom Archives, Jay Mullins, Lisa Roth, Alex Safron
Graphic Designer: Nieves Guerra
Copy Editor: Amy Haejung
Board of Directors: Roberta Arnold, Cheryl Clarke, Julie R. Enszer, Sara Gregory, Yeva Johnson, Shromona Mandal, Joan Nestle, Rose Norman, Mecca Jamilah Sullivan, Yasmin Tambiah, and Red Washburn

Front Cover Art: Graphic
Artist: Lisa Roth • lisarothgrafix.com
Media: Digital design and typography

Biography: Lisa Roth has been a leftist lesbian and graphic designer since the 1960s. She was a founder of the John Brown Anti-Klan Committee and the San Francisco Dyke March.

Artist statement: Free all political prisoners.

Back Cover Art: "Dancing with My Orishas"
Artist: Dylcia Pagán (painter) and Linda Evans (quilter)
Media: Permanent fabric paint and fabric art
Size: 36" × 32"

Artist Statement: Orishas are Yoruba spiritual guides that protect and guide individuals. The larger image is Chango, my six-figure medusa—a warrior woman who dances with powerful movements of rhythms. The others are Yemaya, goddess of the sea; Oya, goddess of the wind and protector of children; and Ochosi, goddess of justice.

SINISTER WISDOM, founded 1976
Former editors and publishers:
Harriet Ellenberger (aka Desmoines) and Catherine Nicholson (1976–1981)
Michelle Cliff and Adrienne Rich (1981–1983)
Michaele Uccella (1983–1984)
Melanie Kaye/Kantrowitz (1983–1987)
Elana Dykewomon (1987–1994)
Caryatis Cardea (1991–1994)
Akiba Onada-Sikwoia (1995–1997)
Margo Mercedes Rivera-Weiss (1997–2000)
Fran Day (2004–2010)
Julie R. Enszer & Merry Gangemi (2010–2013)
Julie R. Enszer (2013–)

Copyright © 2022 *Sinister Wisdom*, Inc.
All rights revert to individual authors and artists upon publication.
Printed in the U. S. on recycled paper.

Subscribe online: www.SinisterWisdom.org
Join *Sinister Wisdom* on Facebook: www.Facebook.com/SinisterWisdom
Follow *Sinister Wisdom* on Instagram: www.Instagram.com/sinister_wisdom
Follow *Sinister Wisdom* on Twitter: www.twitter.com/Sinister_Wisdom
Sinister Wisdom is a US non-profit organization; donations to support the work and distribution of *Sinister Wisdom* are welcome and appreciated.
Consider including *Sinister Wisdom* in your will.

Sinister Wisdom, 2333 McIntosh Road, Dover, FL 33527-5980 USA

DEDICATION

This issue is dedicated to rita bo brown and Marilyn "Mo" Kalman. These two Out of Control members were our close friends and comrades in the struggle for social justice. We miss them both—forever in our hearts.

Photo credit: Susan Goldberg
Courtesy Susan Goldberg

Photo credit: Unknown
Courtesy Etang Inyang

Marilyn "Mo" Kalman
1953–2018

rita bo brown
1947–2021

Mo worked with Out of Control for years and devoted much of her life fighting for political prisoners. As a proud fat activist, working-class dyke, and radical lawyer, Mo defended tenants and produced the SF Dyke March for years.

Bo, ex–political prisoner, freedom fighter, and one of the co-founders of Out of Control, she devoted her life to building the abolition movement. In her own words, she defined herself: "I am an anti-authoritarian lesbian-feminist anarcho-communist."

TABLE OF CONTENTS

Notes for a Magazine 7

BEGINNING: LEXINGTON HIGH SECURITY UNIT AND THE BIRTH OF OUT OF CONTROL

SUSAN ROSENBERG
    Sparks Fly (1987) 10
    Arriving at the High Security Unit 11
ANGELA DAVIS
    Out of Control: Advocating for Freedom Against
        the Carceral State 15
JANE SEGAL AND BROOKE LOBER
    Notes for a Special Issue 21
JANE SEGAL
    Out of Control, Lesbian Committee: Timeline 31

SECTION 1: OUT OF CONTROL: LESBIAN COMMITTEE TO SUPPORT WOMEN POLITICAL PRISONERS (1987–2013)

BLUE MUROV AND JULIE STAROBIN
    Remembering Out of Control 40
SUSAN ROSENBERG
    Out of Control Made a Difference 48
BROOKE LOBER
    Interview with Judith Mirkinson (Mirk) 53
JULIE PERINI
    Bo Brown, the Gentleman Bank Robber 57
    Collage of Bo Brown 61
ANNIE DANGER
    Life is Living 62

Brooke Lober
   Interview with Jane Segal 63
   Interview with Jennifer Beach 69
Chrystos
   "Chowchilla: Gateway to Prosperity" 78

Section 2:
Solidarity with the Puerto Rican Independence Movement

Brooke Lober
   Interview with Frankie Free Ramos 82
Lucy Rodríguez Vélez and Alicia Rodríguez Vélez
   Puerto Rico: Oppression and Resistance 90
Zulma Oliveras Vega
   My Extended Familia 96
Brooke Lober
   Interview with Dylcia Pagán 100

Section 3: FCI Dublin: The Best Kept Secret

Linda Evans
   Remembering Out of Control 109
   When the Prison Doors Are Opened,
      the Real Dragon Will Fly Out 115
Marilyn Buck
   Clandestine Kisses 116
Tanya Napier and Gemma Mirkinson
   For Marilyn Buck (1947–2010) 117
Marilyn Buck
   Moon Bereft 122
   A Story in Celebration of the Intifada 123
Laura Whitehorn
   Scene from the Intifada 124

BROOKE LOBER
    Interview with Judy Siff 125
MARILYN BUCK
    Thirteen Springs 131
BROOKE LOBER
    Interview with Jay Mullins 132
    Out of Control, In Conversation: Judy, Jay, Jane, and Penny 139
LAURA WHITEHORN
    Marilyn Kalman, Out of Control, and "The Codefendants" ... 147
    Woman Dancing 152
    Three Women Musicians 153

SECTION 4: SPARKS FLY

EMILY K. HOBSON
    Fighting HIV/AIDS in Prison 156
KATE RAPHAEL
    Resistance Rises from the Ashes 164
DEBBIE AFRICA
    Note 171
NOELLE HANRAHAN
    Everyone Comes from Somewhere 174
CHRYSTOS
    Going Into the Prison 176
LAURA WHITEHORN
    Cell Portrait 177

LANI KA'AHUMANU
    History Makes Her Own Heroes: A remembrance
        of Sally Miller Gearheart 178

    Book Reviews 195
    Contributors 199

NOTES FOR A MAGAZINE

I am so proud to publish *Sinister Wisdom* 126: *Out of Control* edited by Brooke Lober and Jane Segal. I met Brooke at a National Women's Studies Association conference where she talked about her oral history work with women involved in Out of Control as well as her profound respect and admiration for the activist work of this San Francisco bay area group. Her respect for these activists and commitment to telling their stories enchanted me; I asked her if part of this work might find a home with *Sinister Wisdom*. When we met *Sinister Wisdom* was already in the partnership documenting stories of lesbian-feminist activisms in the South. The story of Out of Control, particularly since it was based in the Bay Area a home of *Sinister Wisdom* in the past, seemed like an excellent next step in this chapter of our history work.

My first conversation with Brooke was nearly ten years ago. It takes time to incubate issues of *Sinister Wisdom*. As you will see reading this issue, the time we put into issues is worth it.

Selections in the issue tell stories about Out of Control and its vital activist work; I am not going to recap it in my introduction, but I do want to share a bit of *Sinister Wisdom's* history and solidarity work with women in prison.

Adrienne Rich and Michelle Cliff were the editors of *Sinister Wisdom* who initiated free subscriptions for women who were in prison or institutionalized. That tradition continues. In the time that I have edited the journal, now about twelve years, we have consistently mailed between 50 and 80 copies of each issue to women on the inside. Women join the list by writing to *Sinister Wisdom* and requesting subscriptions. It is simple. We usually mail them subscriptions until the mail is returned. Many women write to us while inside and after they leave prison to tell us how meaningful the journal is.

In addition for the past two or three years, I have mailed back issues to women in prison on our list. They year, we have received 120 donated copies of *The Sentences that Create Us: Crafting a Writer's Life in Prison*, edited by Caits Meissner, to distribute to lesbians in prison. We will be mailing those books out to women who are in prison over the next year.

I'm proud of the work that *Sinister Wisdom* does in solidarity with women in prison, but I am also aware that our work is miniscule compared to the needs of women—and all people—who are incarcerated. The growing carceral system in the United States is horrific and a form of violence to all people living in this country. I wish that there was more that *Sinister Wisdom* could do and more that I could do to address the individual issues women face—and the systemic issues of carcerality. If you have time and energy, I encourage you to engage in the broad range of activisms to challenge and change our carceral state. Reading *Sinister Wisdom* 126: *Out of Control* may inspire you to engage further in this work. I hope so.

As always, thank you for reading these pages and supporting *Sinister Wisdom*. We are only able to do our small solidarity work with incarcerated women and continue publishing *Sinister Wisdom* because of subscriptions, donations and gifts from readers like you. I hope you will support *Sinister Wisdom* in our fall fundraising campaign. Please give as generously as you can before the end of the year.

In sisterhood,

Julie R. Enszer, PhD
Editor and Publisher, Sinister Wisdom

BEGINNING: LEXINGTON HIGH SECURITY UNIT AND THE BIRTH OF OUT OF CONTROL

SPARKS FLY (1987)

Susan Rosenberg

A calm shuddering deep within
a chill that rises in the midst of dryness
an inner core anger, slowly turning into a fury.

There is no peace without justice
there is no justice without freedom
there is no freedom without dignity and liberation
there is no victory for those who never attempt

When they took us we weren't ready
But—we were more ready than others
We didn't go quietly, but no one stopped them
Some said "they brought it on themselves."
Others "better them than us."
And still others felt the sparks fly
and said we are not lost in the stars.

ARRIVING AT THE HIGH SECURITY UNIT
Susan Rosenberg

We arrived at five in the evening, traveling in jumpsuits and slippers in an eight-seater plane with the marshals. We drove right up to the entrance of the unit and there were hundreds of prisoners' faces at the windows watching. Prisoners had actually been assigned to build the High Security Unit, and it was common knowledge that I was going to be moved there. There were 1,600 prisoners, and the guards took the occasion to lock down the entire prison. One woman screamed out, "Hello, Susan, we know it's you." I started jumping up and down and screamed, "Don't let them bury us down there." Someone else screamed, "We won't." We knew it was going to be underground. It's one thing to know and read; it's another thing to see and experience.

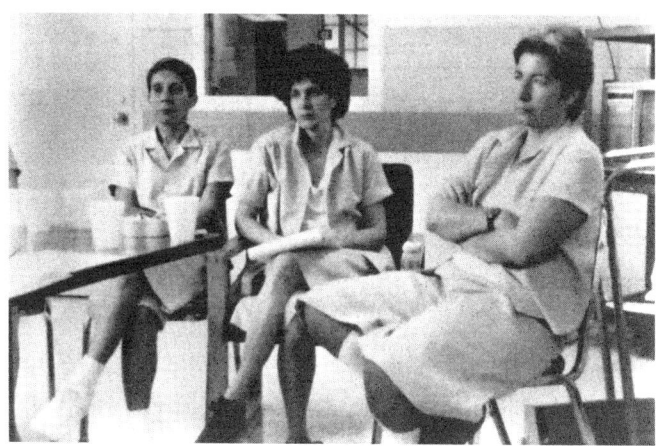

Photo Credit: *On the Issues* 13 (1989); Daedalus Productions
Courtesy Freedom Archives Collection

Left to right: Alejandrina Torres, Susan Rosenberg, and Silvia Baraldini in the High Security Unit for women at Lexington Prison. The HSU's isolation and sensory deprivation were patterned on Stammheim, a supermax prison in Stuttgart, Baden-Württemberg, Germany.

We stood at the electronically controlled metal gate under the eye of one of eleven surveillance cameras. An unidentified man had ordered us placed in restraints while we walked from one end of the basement to the other. The lights were neon, fluorescent, burning, and bright, and everything was snow-white—walls, floors, ceilings. There was no sound except the humming of the lights, and nothing stirred in the air. Alejandrina said, "It's a white tomb, a white sepulcher."

I nodded and whispered, "It's Stammheim."

For nearly three months we were the only prisoners there. We were informed that we were permanently designated to the High Security Unit, expected to serve our entire sentences of thirty-five and fifty-eight years there. We were on constant display. It got so bad that officers would bring their wives and children to tour the unit. A group of high school students came. We made a sign that read "Free all political prisoners in US prisons—stop human rights abuses," and we would display it whenever we heard a tour coming. One day a man toured the unit. He had an Irish accent. As he came on the cell block he said, "So this is the dead wing."

Susan Rosenberg (*Observer Magazine*, May 13, 1988)

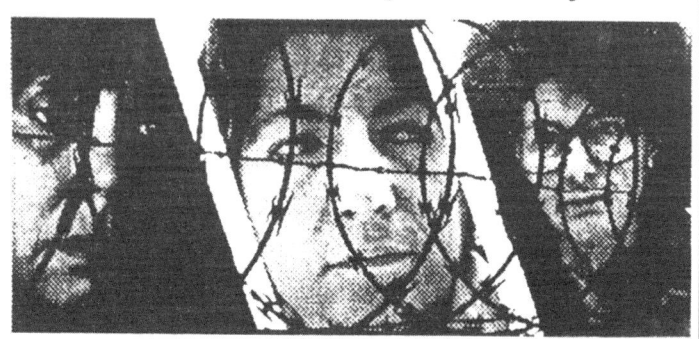

Postcard promoting the 1993 showing of the documentary film *Through The Wire* in San Francisco, California.

OUT OF CONTROL: ADVOCATING FOR FREEDOM AGAINST THE CARCERAL STATE

Angela Davis

Angela Davis

I became acquainted with the work of Out of Control through one of its very early members: Rita "Bo" Brown, a former political prisoner who had been active in the George Jackson Brigade in the Pacific Northwest. We encountered each other in the Bay Area in the late 1980s, when I taught a class at San Francisco State University called "Incarcerated Women." Bo was one of the speakers we asked to participate in the class, around the time that Out of Control launched. I remember her from that time as a vivid, bold and unapologetic working-class, butch lesbian who was relentlessly anti-racist. Over the next decade or so Out of Control invited me to participate in their annual cultural event, "Sparks Fly," along with important feminist cultural workers from the period, Chrystos, Dorothy Allison, Melanie DeMore and others.

Now, forty years later, we find ourselves in a perilous, exciting and strange time; discussions about defunding the police and even abolishing prisons have entered the mainstream in a way that would have been unimaginable only a few years ago. While the police murders of George Floyd and Breonna Taylor were certainly a catalyst for these new developments, a long history of often unacknowledged activism is the real cause.

When we attempt to understand the vastly changed public consciousness regarding prisons and policing, we must recognize the early movement intellectuals and organizers who created the terrain for these changes. Out of Control nurtured many of these radical thinkers and helped to create strong movements, especially powerful campaigns to free political prisoners. These were community scholars—radical lesbians committed to the visibility of lesbians in the community of anti-prison advocates, and the visibility of political prisoners and prisoners of war in the women's community—with a deep understanding of the prison as a repressive tool directed at communities of color and at working-class women of all racial and ethnic backgrounds.

In considering the history of Out of Control, we discover an important thread of resistance that connected the radical lesbian movement of the 1970s, 80s and 90s with the Black Power Movement of the same period. This work was explicitly influenced by key Black Liberation thinkers who were also political prisoners, including Assata Shakur, George Jackson, and Mumia Abu-Jamal.

When I first learned about Out of Control, Lesbian Committee to Shut Down the Lexington Control Unit, the terms "abolition" and "prison industrial complex" had not yet been widely introduced. But the women in this group, many of whom had worked closely with the movement for Black liberation, understood that the violence expressed in prison experiments—like the Lexington High Security Unit—required a demand to shut down, to abolish, not merely to soften its impacts. Their very name rejected reformist approaches and insisted on imagining complete freedom and understood that the freedom of all of us required the freedom of every one of us. Their simultaneous presence in overlapping movements—for freedom to live as lesbians and for freedom from incarceration—signaled that the same systems that were used in the 1950s and 1960s to incarcerate women for lesbian or "deviant" behavior were used in the 1930s, 1960s and 1970s to incarcerate activists, and in the 1980s, 1990s and 2000s to incarcerate substantial portions of black and brown communities.

Out of Control advocated for freedom against the carceral state, mobilizing the feminist movement toward broad, liberatory demands of the internationalist left. Their annual fundraiser "Sparks Fly" simultaneously sought to educate what we then referred to as the "women's community" or "lesbian community" about the existence of women political prisoners in the U.S, to employ culture—mostly poetry and music—to inspire the imagination of these activists, and to directly support women political prisoners by raising money for their commissary funds. This event, along with other activities and a newsletter, "Out of Time," sought to raise consciousness, to demonstrate solidarity and to reach across the prison walls directly to build a resistance movement from within and without. Out of Control understood from its outset that without the aid of people in prison we could not craft a larger analysis of the role of the prison industrial complex.

Out of Control was heavily influenced by the Black and Puerto Rican liberation movements and understood gender to be inherently linked to racist oppressive structures. Composed of formerly incarcerated women and others with close relationships with women still inside, they understood George Jackson's insistence that we not only think of the prison as the site of political repression of people who were engaged in social justice activism in the so called "free world," but we had to try to begin to understand how that apparatus was key to the way racism functioned in our society. These women understood that the same apparatus functioned also to support the oppression—or control—of women and their sexuality. This created an explicit and embedded link between their own insistence on being visible as lesbians in a male-centered movement, and their work to educate the lesbian and queer community about its own relationship to political prisoners, and the need to build relationships with people inside.

The group's feminism and its celebration of lesbian culture was explicitly anti-capitalist, anti-racist, anti-colonial. They were committed to the idea that in being our full authentic selves, and working together, we could build a movement that would imagine and create conditions for all of us to be free. They understood—even before the abolitionist movement explicitly formulated the connection between state violence and intimate violence—that opposing gender violence at an individual level involves opposition to state violence, and that opposing state violence directed at women requires opposing individualized violence against women. They also understood that incarcerating women—the ultimate "control"—was a form of violence connected to individualized gender violence, and that by focusing on these connections, we would more deeply understand the nature of what we later came to call "the prison industrial complex."

Like George Jackson, and so many other intellectuals and leaders who participate in social justice movements from behind bars, Out of Control insisted on a respectful dialog with people inside prisons as they built their work and imagined a movement together.

When Critical Resistance launched a movement against the prison industrial complex in 1998, widening the use of the key phrases "prison industrial complex" and "prison abolition," it did so as a blossoming of several pre-existing movements that all, separately and together, resisted the confines of the state in multiple spheres. Out of Control pre-dated Critical Resistance and contributed to the ground on which it was built. Before the first Critical Resistance conference, radical anti-prison organizing was happening in a wide range of communities, sectors, styles, and locations. There was work with political prisoners, educational work within jails and prisons, and much unrecognized, emergent mutual aid work with women in prison: raising money; maintaining communications; countless hours preparing legal advocacy; and then supporting people upon release. As a small group of unflinching anti-racist, anti-colonial lesbians—some of whom had spent time in prison—Out of Control was an essential part of that largely unrecognized work, particularly on behalf of women: they were part of a large anti-carceral feminist movement that is still generally unacknowledged. In this world of activists who were disinterested in "reform" of prison conditions, and more interested in standing together across communities struggling under the weight of prison oppression, there were these white lesbians who understood that their own marginalization was mandated by the state, and who understood solidarity was our only hope for collective liberation.

Several members of Out of Control served on the organizing committee for the Critical Resistance conference, including Bo Brown, who also facilitated the printing and mass distribution of the now-classic booklet, The Prison Industrial Complex and the Global Economy, written by Eve Goldberg and political prisoner Linda Evans. Out of Control also organized a workshop for Critical Resistance about women political prisoners and prisoners of war, during which women from the Federal Correctional Institution in Dublin CA called in directly to the conference itself, crossing the manufactured divide of prison walls. Out of Control also organized the childcare for Critical Resistance, as part of its support of women's leadership.

Like Critical Resistance, Out of Control saw part of its work as building an anti-racist, anti-capitalist, feminist consciousness among its communities in a way that would now be referred to as "intersectional." The women of Out of Control understood that an amalgam of racist, heteropatriarchal economic, political, cultural, and representational forces were responsible in a complex way for criminalization and imprisonment of people of color, poor people, and queer people. Part of their work, and the way they lived their lives, was to resist those forces by insisting on visibility, demanding freedom, and understanding the urgent necessity of working in concert with people inside to undermine the prison walls. Out of Control demanded visibility for their community of women who had rejected social and political conventions, both for their own authenticity, and because they understood that their ability to be their full authentic selves was in contradiction to a state that used incarceration to control communities.

The women in Out of Control did not work only on shutting down the control unit in Lexington or building a commissary fund to support women political prisoners but also on women's liberation, lesbian visibility, and opposing racism and imperial violence in Puerto Rico, the Philippines, Palestine, and many other places. They did this because they were motivated to understand and build movements based on freedom and self-determination. The personal, in this sense, is the political.

NOTES FOR A SPECIAL ISSUE
Jane Segal and Brooke Lober

The volume that you hold in your hands is priceless. It is a record of the imaginative creations, aspirations, relations, and life histories of the radical lesbian ancestors of our dreams—the organization Out of Control: Lesbian Committee to Support Women Political Prisoners. In the late twentieth century—an era of foreign wars, the rapid growth of the prison industrial complex (PIC), and increasingly alienating consumer culture and technology—this group of self-proclaimed "dykes from hell" convened, bonded, and strengthened. Toward one another, they softened and became steadfast, creating profound friendships and partnerships that formed the building blocks for living their politics in the real world. The members of Out of Control shared a radical stance from which they lived their lives as lesbian, antiracist, feminist abolitionists dedicated to the support of their incarcerated comrades.

From their early days growing up in liberal or conservative homes, most of them radicalized in their teens and twenties, some influenced by the culture of the Jewish left they witnessed in their home communities—this small and remarkable group of women united to support the movements that first inspired them: opposition to the Vietnam War, Black liberation, internationalism, anticolonialism, and indigenous sovereignty. As their decades in these movements became the fabric of their lives, they would soon spend many years largely focused on their close friends and comrades who had been incarcerated for acts of armed resistance, held on disproportionate charges for being "too radical," and, in the worst cases, subjected to torture, abuse, and many violations of civil and human rights. Out of Control fought back. In advocating publicly for their radical sisters inside, from the 1980s into the 2000s, Out of Control embodied an important nexus of several social movements: the prison movement of the late twentieth century, the emerging movement for the abolition of the prison industrial complex of the early 2000s, the gay liberation movement, queer and trans culture and politics, and leftist internationalism.

On these pages, you will meet the members of this remarkable group. Jane, Jay, Judy, Julie, Blue, Mo, and bo were the core, long-term members of Out of Control. For a generation, this wild bunch were more than political comrades: they were heartfelt friends and family. Co-conspirators including Mirk, Penny, Jennifer, Leslie, Rachel, Buss, Diane, Madeline, and others who do or don't make an appearance here joined the group for different lengths of time. Over the past five years, former members of Out of Control have collaborated with movement scholar Brooke Lober to record a herstory: a careful tracing of the life of this organization in the words of its members, with contributions from many comrades, former political prisoners, and a few fellow travelers. Much of this volume consists of interviews, along with photos and flyers from the personal archives of Out of Control members, selected and edited by Jane Segal.

In "Beginnings: The Lexington High Security Unit and the Birth of Out of Control," we introduce Out of Control, born in a moment of crisis. Silvia Baraldini, who had participated in radical movements since her undergraduate days at the University of Wisconsin–Madison, was apprehended in 1982, convicted of conspiracy to free Assata Shakur, and subsequently held in the Federal Correctional Institution, Dublin (FCI Dublin), in the Bay Area. There, her friends who lived locally, including Jane Segal, Jay Mullins, and Judith Mirkinson (Mirk), could often visit. When, in 1987, Silvia was secretly transferred from FCI Dublin to a new high-security unit built in the basement of the Lexington, Kentucky federal prison, alongside fellow political prisoners Susan Rosenberg and Alejandrina Torres, the movement collectively shuddered. Women who had been friends and comrades of so many, apprehended for their participation in acts of militancy, were now incarcerated in a gleaming white high-tech facility for solitary confinement, small group isolation, and constant surveillance.

The Lexington Control Unit, Lexington HSU, or simply "Lexington" was created in an era characterized by an unceasing succession of shocking acts and revelations of counterinsurgency targeting radicals and the communities they came from with licit and illicit means for demobilizing and destroying movements. The more they found out about the Lexington Control Unit, the more alarmed activists became. A campaign was launched to free the women from the Lexington HSU, spearheaded by the Movimiento de Liberación Nacional (MLN). A national organizing effort formed, with the National Committee to Free the Puerto Rican Prisoners of War, the United Methodist Church, the United Church of Christ, the ACLU, and many others, as well as Out of Control, all remaining members of the coalition until the HSU closed.[1]

Committee to Shut Down Lexington Control Unit created and performed a guerrilla theater piece at Gay Pride and other events to demonstrate opposition to conditions at Lexington HSU.

Design Credit: Out of Control
Courtesy Out of Control Collection

Beginning with their exposure of the Lexington HSU in flyers, pamphlets, street theater, protest marches, and at LGBTQ and feminist community events, Out of Control claimed that political prisoners were being unjustly targeted, punished for their political

---

1 See Susan Rosenberg, *An American Radical: Political Prisoner in My Own Country* (Kensington Publishing Corporation, 2011).

views, and subjected to torture in the United States—and some of this torture happened in gendered ways. As member Jennifer Beach recalls, the group believed "that there are particular ways that the state tries to control women and uses women as kind of guinea pigs." Activists across the movement stressed the deplorable conditions the women were held in and argued that they were being punished for their political beliefs. In a pamphlet created for the National Campaign to Abolish the Lexington Women's Control Unit, activists wrote, "Lexington is a behavior modification unit characterized by systematic use of sensory deprivation, extreme isolation and degradation."[2]

While the facility was still open, radical scholar Gilda Zwerman wrote the following:

The HSU at Lexington reflects the emergence of a new strategy in neoclassical correctional philosophy which may be determined "special incapacitation," that is, isolation with intensive surveillance and sensory deprivation. Its purpose is to contain and monitor primarily (though not exclusively) women political prisoners.

The importance of examining the HSU as an emergent correctional strategy is three-fold:

1. It utilizes and manipulates the "terrorist" label, as defined by conservative ideologues, in order to justify the "special" treatment of political prisoners within the correctional system;
2. It demonstrates how intelligence and counterinsurgency policies may be infused into the correctional system; and

---

[2] National Campaign to Abolish the Lexington Women's Control Unit, "Buried Alive in the Lexington Women's Control Unit," pamphlet, 1989. Available at the Freedom Archives: http://www.freedomarchives.org/Documents/Finder/DOC510_scans/Lexington/510.buried.alive.lexington.womens.control.1989.pdf

3. It represents an expansion in the use of incapacitation, surveillance, and deterrence as mechanisms for social control and repression to a degree heretofore unprecedented in the US correctional system.[3]

Zwerman argues that the Lexington HSU was indeed a torture unit, an intensification of counterrevolutionary state practice developed in the two Reagan administrations. The claim of state torture became a major strategy in the public campaign and legal case to close the Lexington HSU, which was condemned as a "living tomb" by the ACLU and Amnesty International.[4] While the activists did win the closure of the Lexington HSU, to their rage and dismay, their sisters would be transferred to other control units, beginning with the Shawnee unit at the Federal Correctional Institution in Marianna, Florida, which was opened in 1988.[5] The landmark ruling, that the women could not be held in the unit for their political views, was overturned. The state practice of high-security control units increased, and "maximum-security" or "supermax" prisons with the capacity for sustained mass solitary confinement became common across the United States, with at least thirty operating by the turn of the millennium.[6] As the PIC massified, the ongoing campaigns for release of these same women political prisoners, along with their friends and comrades,

---

[3] Gilda Zwerman, "Special Incapacitation: The Emergence of a New Correctional Facility for Women Political Prisoners," *Social Justice* 15, no. 1 (1988): 31–47.

[4] See Amnesty International, "Summary, United States: The High Security Unit, Lexington Federal Prison, Kentucky," August 1988. http://freedomarchives. org/Documents/Finder/DOC510_scans/Lexington/510.amnesty.international. lexington.hsu.summary.1988.pdf.

[5] Silvia Baraldini, Marilyn Buck, Laura Whitehorn, and Susan Rosenberg, "Women's Control Unit: Marianna, FL." http://freedomarchives.org/Documents/Finder/DOC4_scans/4.womens.control.unit.1992.pdf

[6] Leena Kurki and Norval Morris, "The Purposes, Practices, and Problems of Supermax Prisons," *Crime and Justice* 28 (2001).

became the space of action for this radical lesbian committee that would last for the next quarter-century.

For the following decades, Out of Control's work took the form of mutual aid: direct support for the incarcerated women through fundraising and legal support for their cases, communications though their newsletter *Out of Time*, and also through personal visits and the creation of the strongest social bonds—both friendship and family. They tirelessly represented the conditions of the incarcerated women, thereby exposing repressive state practice and magnetizing queer and feminist publics to the causes of anti-imperialism, anticolonialism, and antiracism for which the incarcerated women had taken up arms in the first place.

The major event for Out of Control was a yearly fundraiser for the Women Political Prisoner Commissary Fund. Named "Sparks Fly" after Susan Rosenberg's expression of the "sparks" that could fly between the bars—inspiring communication with otherwise isolated, incarcerated comrades—the cultural and educational event gathered feminist publics to support their cause. As Kate Raphael, friend of Out of Control and founding member of LAGAI (Lesbians and Gays Against Intervention) writes in this volume, their yearly garage sale in the Castro, San Francisco's gay community, supported the Women Political Prisoner Commissary Fund while providing a space for connection in a community that was devastated by the AIDS crisis. Over the years, Out of Control supported the five Puerto Rican women prisoners of war who were apprehended in their struggle to topple US colonialism. They additionally supported the incarcerated women of the MOVE organization, also with commissary funds. And while their newsletter and the many events they produced focused on women political prisoners—emphasizing the necessity to do so to address the specific conditions they faced—Out of Control also directly supported and drew attention to international and US political prisoners of all genders.

In 1988, political prisoners Marilyn Buck, Linda Evans, Susan Rosenberg, Timothy Blunk, Alan Berkman, Laura Whitehorn, and Elizabeth Duke were indicted in what activists called the "Resistance Conspiracy" case. This indictment was the right-wing administration's response to a series of anti-imperialist acts of armed propaganda. As archivists at the Freedom Archives explain, the series of bombings, meant to exact extreme property damage but not to hurt anyone, targeted "US foreign aggression: the invasion of Grenada; the US role in arming the Contra army in Nicaragua; supporting dictatorships in El Salvador, Guatemala, and Honduras; the colonization of Puerto Rico since 1898; support of the Israeli occupation of Palestine; support of apartheid in South Africa; and police brutality and anti-Black racism in the United States."[7] When the codefendants were sent to federal prison in Washington, DC (except Elizabeth Duke, who escaped), members of Out of Control offered material support. As Laura Whitehorn writes in this volume, the self-taught movement lawyer Mo Kalman, a member of Out of Control, temporarily moved to DC to offer legal, social, and even spiritual support for the codefendants.

As the case of the Resistance Conspiracy's lesbian political prisoners became known to movement activists, worlds sometimes collided. The popular lesbian cartoonist Alison Bechdel featured the women political prisoners among the Resistance Conspiracy defendants in an episode of her serial comic "Dykes to Watch Out For." But, as Jane explains in the group interview included here, most attendees of the Dyke March and Gay Pride didn't know about the women featured on the signs carried by Out of Control members. In order to inform and educate the feminist and LGBTQ community about this case, Out of Control distributed note cards and poetry booklets, created by and benefitting the Resistance Conspiracy defendants. Through decades of coalition organizing, as visible dykes in leftist formations united in their will to free their comrades, Out of Control made friends and allies, overturning

---

[7] "Resistance Conspiracy: Finding Aid," The Freedom Archives, accessed January 26, 2022, https://search.freedomarchives.org/search.php?view_collection=325.

homophobic practices and viewpoints within the movement. Promoting the causes of political prisoners to feminist and queer publics, Out of Control also resisted the turn to neoliberal inclusion and embodied a queer and feminist politics of racial and economic justice, and opposition to US imperialism at home and abroad.

As section two of this volume shows, Out of Control's local work contributed to an internationalist anticolonial effort. When prominent members of the Puerto Rican liberation struggle were incarcerated at FCI Dublin, their Bay Area location brought movement groups and individuals into closer relation. In this period, as activist Frankie Free Ramos explains, Out of Control collaborated with supporters of the Puerto Rican women prisoners to raise funds and get the word out about the incarcerated radical women. In 1992, Out of Control participated in the International Tribunal of Indigenous Peoples and Oppressed Nations in the USA, which put the United States on trial, finding the state guilty of war crimes, genocide, and incarceration of political prisoners, among other charges.[8]

As sections three and four demonstrate, while Out of Control remained a participant in the organized left, committed to the release of political prisoners, their activism overspilled the boundary between the defense of political prisoners and the movement to combat the growing PIC as a whole. Out of Control members helped to organize the first Critical Resistance conference in 1998 and offered a workshop in which women political prisoners phoned into the conference—one of the few spaces where currently incarcerated people were able to speak live at this pivotal event.

In their group interview in this volume, members of Out of Control consider the dynamics between work to free political prisoners and efforts to combat the PIC as a whole. As they

---

8 "Verdict of the International Tribunal of Indigenous Peoples and Oppressed Nations in the USA," October 4, 1992, The Freedom Archives, http://freedomarchives.org/Documents/Finder/DOC35_scans/35.1992tribunal.verdict.english.pdf.

remember, the two aspects of the prison movement sometimes clashed, and there continues to be a sense that the causes of political prisoners are not as highlighted in abolitionist spaces as some feel they ought to be. As Judy Siff states in this volume, "We don't want to ever forget the political prisoners, and they do get forgotten. I mean, you might want to notice when you go places where prisoners have been talked about. See if the political prisoners are mentioned or not. Mostly, I would say, not." In 1990, the young butch lesbian activist Noelle Hanrahan co-produced a radio series with members of Out of Control and other activists to amplify the causes and cases of political prisoners and the PIC. Hanrahan writes that "Out of Control shaped the entire culture" of radical queer activism, inspiring her, as a young butch lesbian, to take up the cause of political prisoners. For over thirty years, Hanrahan has continued to lead the Prison Radio project, which has powerfully affected social movements by bringing the voice of political prisoner Mumia Abu-Jamal to the airwaves.

In practical terms, mounting resistance against the prison system as a state tactic to demobilize the left *and* to oppress marginalized communities meant that at times, Out of Control joined defense campaigns for incarcerated people who were referred to as "social prisoners"—those who were targeted by criminalization, not incarcerated for deliberate acts of political resistance. For example, for many years, Out of Control circulated petitions, fundraised by selling T-shirts, gained support by direct appeal in *Out of Time*, and advocated for the release of Norma Jean Croy, a Native American woman who was pursued by the FBI and wrongly convicted. In this campaign and in much of their work, Out of Control exceeded the cause of political prisoner support, to emphasize the political nature of the prison itself.

Out of Control, and their comrades inside, advocated for the dignity and rights of all incarcerated people. Sometimes, this took the form of supporting AIDS activism in prison: incarcerated activists Susan Rosenberg, Laura Whitehorn, and Marilyn Buck did AIDS education and organizing while they were incarcerated in a maximum-security unit in Marianna, Florida. And Linda Evans, Marilyn Buck, and Laura Whitehorn organized for the AIDS walkathon and the NAMES Project AIDS Memorial Quilt when they were together in FCI Dublin. As Whitehorn writes, half of the women in the prison eventually participated in the walkathon, which Out of Control raised support for and publicized beyond the walls. As scholar Emily Hobson writes in this volume, AIDS activism among political prisoners constituted some of the most powerful and exemplary work of this generation of revolutionaries.

From a local base in the Bay Area, Out of Control's reach extended across the world as they supported international political prisoners from Palestine to Ireland. As feminist activists, their reach also extended into the intimacies of gender relations, as they raised consciousness and movement support for women who were criminalized after they killed abusers in acts of self-defense. After the Puerto Rican prisoners of war and several of the white anti-imperialist political prisoners were released in 1999 and 2001, members of Out of Control maintained friendships and continued their movement activity. They continued advocating vigorously for Marilyn Buck, who was not released until 2010. They also continued to advocate for and report on the primarily Black political prisoners who remained incarcerated by a racist state. Even after the group's official work ended, Out of Control remained a community. Some continued organizing against the PIC and on behalf of political prisoners, and provided care and support for activist comrades who faced health conditions while aging. Two of those comrades, Mo and bo, passed away while this project was being created. In these pages, they rejoin their sisters, the "dykes from hell" whose legacy still sparks and burns so bright.

OUT OF CONTROL, LESBIAN COMMITTEE: TIMELINE

Jane Segal

1956: The US Federal Government launches a domestic counterintelligence program, COINTELPRO, that targets political activists and organizations and implements a wide range of strategies to dismantle them and make them ineffective. Those strategies include aggressive approaches to arrests, trials, and prison conditions. The hope is that by tying up movement resources in lengthy court cases and by torturing leaders through harsh prison conditions, social justice movements will falter. This approach impacts marginalized communities more intensely. The Black liberation movement, the Black Panthers, the Puerto Rican independence movement, and Native American organizations suffer the most dramatic consequences. Women and lesbians are targeted for especially grueling conditions.

1970: Angela Davis is arrested. August 14, 1970: The Marin County court issues a warrant for Angela Davis' arrest. Within four days of the warrant, the FBI places her on their Ten Most Wanted Fugitive List, launching a massive search for her. In response, a national and international campaign works tirelessly to support Angela Davis and fight for her freedom. October 13, 1970, she is captured and arrested. An international movement rises to fight for her freedom. June 4, 1972, she is found not guilty of all charges after a highly politicized trial.

1971: George Jackson is murdered in San Quentin State Prison, San Quentin, California.

1973: Assata Shakur, former Black Panther and member of the Black Liberation Army, is arrested. Shakur is a target of the FBI's COINTELPRO counterintelligence program. She is acquitted of several felonies. In 1977 she is convicted of assault with intent to kill a New Jersey state trooper and incarcerated at Clinton Correctional Facility for Women, New Jersey.

Circa 1978: The Federal Bureau of Prisons opens Davis Hall, a high-security unit for women within the Federal Prison Camp, Alderson (FPC Alderson), West Virginia. Lolita Lebrón, Assata Shakur, and rita "bo" brown are incarcerated in that unit.

1979: Assata is liberated from her isolation cell in the Clinton Correctional Facility for Women, in New Jersey.

1978–97: Norma Jean Croy and her brother Patrick "Hooty" Croy are arrested in 1978 and convicted in 1979 of murder, conspiracy, and assault. A Shasta-Karok woman and a lesbian, Norma is sentenced to life in prison although she wasn't carrying a gun, never fired a shot. The case is marred by anti-Native prejudice in Northern California. She spends nineteen years in prison until her conviction is overturned in 1996 and she is released in 1997. Out of Control publicizes Norma's case in *Out of Time*, cosponsors a benefit for Norma and the International Tribunal of Indigenous Peoples and Oppressed Nations in the USA in 1992, organizes letters to the parole board, and supports her after her release.

1984–85: The Federal Bureau of Prisons (BOP) opens the Cardinal Unit, a pre-high-security experimental unit, at FPC Alderson, WV. The Cardinal Unit uses electronically monitored cages to house Puerto Rican political prisoner Marie Haydée Beltrán Torres and Puerto Rican POW Lucy Rodríguez Vélez. They are isolated and confined to their cells twenty-four hours a day for close to one year. Their assignment to this unit is due to their political beliefs and associations as Puerto Rican Independentistas.

October 29, 1986: The Bureau of Prisons opens the female High Security Unit (HSU) within the Federal Correctional Institution, Lexington (FCI Lexington), Kentucky. The HSU is a subterranean behavior-modification unit in the basement of a high-security building, separate from the rest of the federal prison. This "prison within a prison," an extreme isolation unit with a cost of approximately $735,000, was specifically built to house women political prisoners and Puerto Rican prisoners of war. The conditions amount to psychological torture. Alejandrina Torres, Puerto Rican Independentista and self-proclaimed prisoner of war, and Susan Rosenberg, anti-imperialist North American political prisoner, are transferred to the Lexington HSU for Women. According to attorney Jan Susler of the People's Law Office, Chicago, Illinois, the three women initially transferred—Susan Rosenberg, Alejandrina Torres, and Silvia Baraldini—"had no record of posing a security threat in prison, but instead were political activists affiliated with radical groups."[1]

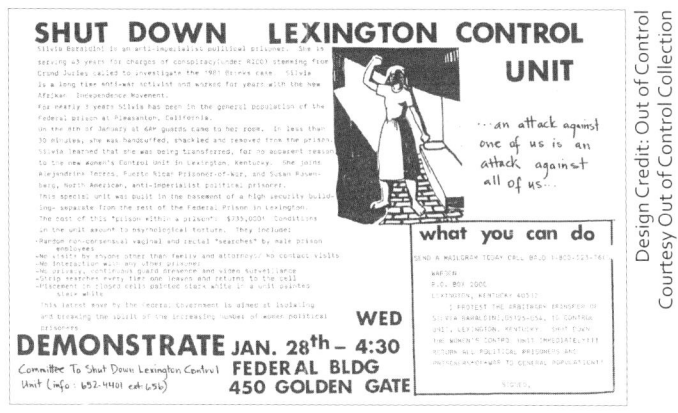

Committee to Shut Down Lexington Control Unit, later known as Out of Control: Lesbian Committee to Support Women Political Prisoners, held their first action at the San Francisco Federal Building. 1987.

January 8, 1987: Silvia Baraldini, Italian national and anti-imperialist political prisoner, is transferred to the Lexington HSU for Women.

January 1987: Four activists—three lesbians and one straight woman, all friends of Silvia Baraldini and other women political

---

1 Jan Susler, "The Women's High Security Unit in Lexington, KY," *Yale Journal of Law and Liberation* 1, no. 1 (1989): 32.

prisoners—meet to plan a response to the Bureau of Prisons' newest HSU for women and the abrupt transfer of Silvia Baraldini to the HSU to join Susan Rosenberg and Alejandrina Torres. Former political prisoner rita bo brown, Jay Mullins, Jane Segal, and Judith Mirkinson (Mirk) form the Committee to Shut Down Lexington Control Unit.

January 28, 1987: The Committee to Shut Down Lexington Control Unit holds its first action at the Federal Building, 450 Golden Gate, San Francisco. The activists' call to action is: an attack against one of us is an attack against all of us.

Summer 1987–August 1988: The Puerto Rican independence group Movimiento de Liberación Nacional (MLN) initiates and leads the fight to close the HSU. The National Campaign to Abolish the Lexington Women's Control Unit includes a wide array of social justice groups, from churches to radical women and lesbian groups. Out of Control joins and remains a member organization until the HSU is closed.

Summer 1987–August 1988: While working with the National Campaign to Abolish the Lexington Women's Control Unit, Out of Control organizes locally in the San Francisco women's/lesbian/gay community: educating with literature, writing articles, collecting thousands of letters of protest about the Lexington unit, and performing a guerrilla theater piece about the horrors of the HSU. Out of Control organizes the publication of a full-page ad protesting the control unit in *Gay Community News*, Boston, Massachusetts, and *Off Our Backs*, Washington, DC. Working with other lesbian organizations from Chicago, New York, and Lexington, they reach out to prominent members and organizations in the women's, lesbian, and gay communities and publish the protest ads circa May 1988.

October 1987: The Federal Bureau of Prisons announces it will close Lexington and move its mission to a new, larger women's prison in Marianna, Florida. Despite the announcement, the Bureau of Prisons does not close the HSU until August 1988.

1988: A lawsuit is filed on behalf of Silvia Baraldini, Susan Rosenberg, and Sylvia Brown by the American Civil Liberties Union's National Prison Project (Washington, DC), the Center for Constitutional Rights (New York, NY), Peoples Law Office (Chicago, IL), and private lawyers challenging regulations allowing the small-group isolation and sensory deprivation of prisoners based on their political beliefs or affiliations.

July 15, 1988: Federal judge Barrington Parker in Washington, DC, orders that political prisoners Susan Rosenberg and Silvia Baraldini be transferred into general population. He bars the Bureau of Prisons from "considering a prisoner's past political association or personal political beliefs" in deciding federal prison assignments. An unprecedented ruling, a federal court says in the clearest terms that the US government holds political prisoners and cruelly violates their human rights.

August 15, 1988: The Lexington HSU is officially shut down after almost two years. Susan Rosenberg and Silvia Baraldini are moved to a newly built BOP high-security unit called the Shawnee Unit at the Federal Correctional Institution, Marianna (FCI Marianna), Marianna, FL. Alejandrina Torres is moved to FCI Danbury, Connecticut.

1988–90: In what becomes known as the Resistance Conspiracy case, six defendants face conspiracy charges for "using illegal means to influence, change, and protest policies and practices of the US government"; the US government "admit[s] that there [is] "no direct proof that the individual activists were involved in the bombings, rather [uses] conspiracy charges to convict them."[2]

1989–2013: *Out of Time*, Out of Control's newsletter and primary educational tool, is published as a double-sided xeroxed page and grows into a tabloid-size, four-page newsletter, distributed alone and as an insert inside *UltraViolet*, Lesbian and

---

2 "Resistance Conspiracy: Finding Aid," The Freedom Archives, accessed January 26, 2022, https://search.freedomarchives.org/search.php?view_collection=325.

Gay Intervention's (LAGAI) newsletter. Published four to five times a year, *Out of Time* reports on the cases and struggles of national and international political prisoners, with a primary focus on women. Other newsletter spotlights include battered women in prison for defending themselves, LGBT prisoners, prison abolition, and the significant growth of the US prison industrial complex. When Norma Jean Croy is released in 1997, *Out of Time*'s front page reflects that joyous event. There is a celebratory issue in 1999 after the release of most of the Puerto Rican POWs.

September 8, 1989: The US Court of Appeals in Washington, DC, overturns the Barrington Parker decision, saying the government is free to use the political beliefs and associations of prisoners as a basis and reason for placing them in maximum security.

1989–2010: The first Sparks Fly event is an International Day of Solidarity with Women Political Prisoners and commemorates the liberation of political prisoner Assata Shakur on November 2, 1979. Sparks Fly is an annual cultural and political event highlighting poets and musicians as it raises consciousness about women political prisoners and raises funds for the Women Political Prisoners Commisary Fund. It is a community celebration and an educational event collaboratively organized by Out of Control, Women Against Imperialism, LAGAI, and individual activists.

1990: Out of Control and LAGAI launch the Women Political Prisoner Commissary Fund because prisoners must buy everything they want or need at the commissary, including shampoo, aspirin, dental floss, and more. Prisoners must also buy their own stamps and phone calls, so communication with family and friends depends on individuals' commissary accounts.

October 2–4, 1992: The International Tribunal of Indigenous Peoples and Oppressed Nations in the USA convenes in San Francisco, CA. Marilyn "Mo" Kalman, Esq., a member of Out of Control, presents the case of the white North American political prisoners by taking testimony from rita bo brown, former political prisoner and member of Out of Control. The brief, presented on behalf of Out of Control and Prairie Fire Organizing Committee, outlines the violations of international law regarding the treatment of white North American political prisoners.

September 25–27, 1998: Critical Resistance: Beyond the Prison Industrial Complex, a national conference and strategy session at the University of California, Berkeley, examines and challenges mass incarceration and policing. Over 3,500 people attend; the range of people includes formerly and currently incarcerated people, their families, activists, academics, unhoused people, policymakers, feminists, and gay, lesbian, and trans activists. Critical Resistance recognizes the work has just begun. Their mission: to build an international movement to challenge the prison industrial complex. The conference, initiated by Angela Davis, Ruth Wilson Gilmore, and Rose Braz, is a success. Out of Control has two members on the organizing committee, and presents a workshop on women political prisoners called "Sparks Fly." Several women political prisoners from FCI-Dublin call in to the workshop. Out of Control produces and distributes a booklet, also called *Sparks Fly*, featuring all the women political prisoners and POWs. They also distribute a booklet by Eve Goldberg and Linda Evans, called "The Prison Industrial Complex and the Global Economy."

1999: A big year to celebrate!

1999: Out of Control publishes the *SF Ironical*: *Best Kept Secret.* The *Ironical* is a poster that looks much like the *SF Chronicle* daily paper and highlights the reality that seven women political prisoners and POWs are incarcerated at FCI Dublin, California. Activists carefully coordinated an action, placing the poster into the *SF Chronicle* newspaper vending machines.

1999: Susan Crane and Donna Howard-Hastings, Plowshares prisoners of conscience, are freed from prison after completing their sentences for disarmament actions against US nuclear missiles.

August 6, 1999: Laura Whitehorn is released after spending over fourteen years in federal prison.

August 24, 1999: After a ten-year campaign, Silvia Baraldini is transferred by the US Justice Department to an Italian prison.

September 10, 1999: After nineteen years behind bars, Dylcia Pagán, Alicia and Lucy Rodríguez Vélez, Alejandrina Torres, and Carmen Valentín, along with six compañeros, are granted conditional parole by President Bill Clinton.

2001: Linda Evans is released from prison after sixteen and a half years.

2001: Susan Rosenberg is released from prison after seventeen years.

2010: A group of activists produce the final Sparks Fly event, in honor of Marilyn Buck and all women political prisoners.

2013: The final issue of *Out of Time* is published.

2017: A collaboration of people, including former Out of Control members, produce a benefit for bo brown.

SECTION 1: OUT OF CONTROL: LESBIAN COMMITTEE TO SUPPORT WOMEN POLITICAL PRISONERS (1987–2013)

REMEMBERING OUT OF CONTROL
Blue Murov and Julie Starobin

We dedicate this article to the memory of three of our friends: Marilyn Buck, ex–political prisoner; bo brown, cofounder of Out of Control, ex–political prisoner; and Mo Kalman, longtime movement lawyer and activist.

"Shut down the Lexington Control Unit!" This was the catalyst for bringing us together in January of 1987 to form the group that was first called Committee to Shut Down the Lexington Control Unit. We were lesbians and straight women who had been doing prisoner support work for a decade. Some of us were former political prisoners, and a few of us knew the three women political prisoners, Alejandrina Torres, Silvia Baraldini, and Susan Rosenberg, who were being held in Lexington, KY. "Shutting down the Control Unit" quickly became a national movement led by many different organizations, lawyers, and faith-based groups. A lawsuit brought against the Federal Bureau of Prisons by the ACLU was won, and the unit was closed eighteen months after it opened.

A political prisoner is anyone incarcerated because of their self-conscious political actions against the government. We do not consider people who are in prison for right-wing actions to be political prisoners. Women have been imprisoned for the following acts:

- providing sanctuary for Central American refugees
- antinuclear and antimilitary actions
- self-defense against sexual abuse
- fighting for Black liberation
- defending land and treaty rights of Native peoples
- refusing to testify before a grand jury in a government investigation

- fighting for the independence of Puerto Rico from the US
- defending the rights of lesbians and gay men

There were over 100 self-identified political prisoners in US prisons in 1987, so we decided to keep doing the work, as a group, to support twenty-five women political prisoners and other incarcerated, especially lesbians, when and where we found them. We changed our name to Out of Control: Lesbian Committee to Support Women Political Prisoners. Part of our work was to fight against lesbian invisibility—not only for ourselves, but also for our lesbian sisters inside.

One of our first projects in 1989 was a newsletter. Bo brown, a founding member and former political prisoner, had a saying: "Time flies when you're not doing it." This inspired the name for our newsletter, *Out of Time*. With over a million people and growing in US prisons, it felt like we were out of time, and we wanted to help people get out of jail (doing time). *Out of Time* was the perfect vehicle to bring the issue of political prisoners to LGBTQ communities and to bring the issue of lesbian liberation to other movements and communities. Some of us learned desktop publishing, we found a union printer, and we were on our way with a newsletter that lasted more than twenty years.

Starting in June 1989, we produced *Out of Time* four to five times a year, free to all. It was mailed separately and as the centerfold of *UltraViolet*, the newsletter of LAGAI (currently LAGAI–Queer Insurrection). Over the years, even as our mailing list grew and grew, more than half were people inside. Though *Out of Time* is no more, *UltraViolet* is still being published by LAGAI four times a year and includes many articles by and about prisoners in this country and the world. Still free, their subscriber list is now over 3,300; 2,800 are incarcerated people.[1]

---

1 www.lagai.org.

Out of Time grew into a tabloid-size newsletter and featured US and international political prisoners, focusing on the women. This issue focuses on Palestinian women prisoners and Leonard Peltier's nomination for the Nobel Peace Prize.

Out of Time was one of our ways of reaching out to our LGBTQ community. There were articles about political prisoners and about women in prison for fighting back against abuse. Letters from inside and articles written by us challenged the conditions in prison and asked for support. We always tried to have information at the end of the articles about "things to do," ways to help. We had information about demonstrations, local and global. *Out of Time* publicized national and international campaigns doing advocacy for battered women, anti–death penalty work, prison abolition, and the growth of the prison industrial complex. We highlighted issues that affected lesbians in prison and printed letters asking for help. We also included resources, especially for LGBTQ prisoners; good news when possible; and political rants when appropriate.

> **OUT OF TIME**
>
> Issue No. 6 — Out of Control--Lesbian Committee to Support Women Political Prisoners — September 1990
>
> ## FREE NORMA JEAN CROY!
>
> Norma Jean Croy, a Shasta Indian and a lesbian, is in prison for murder even though she wasn't carrying a gun and never fired a shot. Patrick "Hooty" Croy, her brother, Jaspar Alford, a cousin, and she were convicted of killing a police officer in 1978. Both Patrick and Norma Jean were shot in the back by police during the incident in Siskyou County, CA. Patrick received the death penalty, Jaspar served 8 eight years, and Norma got life.
>
> In May 1990 in San Francisco, Patrick Croy was freed from death row by an excellent defense team that included Native American people. They told a tale of terror, anti-Indian racism, and Native Americans being hunted down and shot in the back by out-of-control police. Evidence presented in Patrick's retrial but withheld from Norma's original trial showed that the fatally wounded police officer had a high blood alcohol level. The jury found that the incident was provoked by racism toward Native Americans in the Yreka area, and that police misconduct led to the officer's death.
>
> The presentation of a cultural defense on behalf of Native Peoples is a long time coming in u.s. courts. Sentences against Native Americans are longer and many times more severe than sentences against whites for the same crimes. In several states Native American children are not allowed the "benefits" of juvenile hall, and are placed in adult prisons.
>
> Norma Jean has spent 12 years as a hostage of the u.s. government in a California prison. She says the outcome of her trial in 1978 was just a continuation of the discrimination and unfair treatment that she experienced all her life. She has been before the parole board four times, the latest being in May--two weeks after her brother's acquittal. At that hearing Norma Jean was denied parole despite pleas for her release by Patrick's legal defense, the recommendation of the California Superior judge who ruled on Patrick's retrial, and support from many concerned individuals.
>
> Patrick's defense attorneys are committing themselves to freeing Norma Jean. Funds are needed for community support activities, publicity and for her personal needs. Send your support to:
>
> Free Norma Jean Croy Defense Committee
> 473 Jackson St.
> San Francisco, CA 94111
> (415) 986-5591
> You can write to Norma Jean Croy #14293 at LBRM 322u, Frontera, CA 91720.
>
> Out of Control will continue to publicize information about Norma Jean's case and fight for her retrial and release.
>
> ### RESISTANCE CONSPIRACY CONTINUES
>
> The defendants in the Resistance Conspiracy case have reached a plea agreement with the u.s. government. All charges will be dismissed against Alan Berkman, Tim Blunk and Susan Rosenberg; they have already been convicted of conspiracy in earlier trials and could argue that this case constituted double jeopardy. Marilyn Buck, Linda Evans and Laura Whitehorn will plead guilty to conspiracy and the Capitol bombing;they will get 15 years each. Laura will also plead guilty to one of the five counts in her outstanding Baltimore indictment and get another 5 for that.
>
> The actual plea will be presented to the judge on September 7, and sentencing will be in the middle of October.
>
> The plea negotiations were prompted by Alan's recurrence of cancer. With the Resistance Conspiracy Case charges dismissed, Alan has a much better chance of winning parole and recuperating from chemotherapy on the Outside. The letter writing campaign for Alan's parole continues.
>
> A petition campaign around the sentencing of Marilyn, Laura and Linda is also under way. Linda (an esteemed Dyke From Hell) is already doing 35 years for buying 4 legal guns with false I.D. Marilyn is doing 70 years. Like all political prisoners, their sentences are outrageously long
>
> *cont. on next page*
>
> Published by Out of Control — Box 30, 3543 18th St., San Francisco, CA 94110

Design Credit: Out of Control
Courtesy Out of Control Collection

Out of Control's primary educational tool was *Out of Time*. First published in 1989 as a double-sided xeroxed page. This sample features Norma Jean Croy, a Shasta-Karok lesbian, unjustly incarcerated for murder. It also features the Resistance Conspiracy defendants: six political activists, three of whom were lesbians, on trial for political conspiracy charges.

By 2001, many of the women political prisoners in the US had been released, though many still remained. We expanded our coverage of women political prisoners internationally, from Palestine to Haiti to Peru, from the Philippines to Turkey. In 2005 we started a very popular and successful lesbian pen pal column. Lesbians inside would send small descriptions along with their addresses, looking for people to write them. Communication with the outside world is very important to every prisoner and *Out of Time* tried to facilitate that in all ways.

In 1990, Out of Control and LAGAI started the Women Political Prisoner Commissary Fund because we wanted to provide some kind of material support to the twenty-five women political prisoners and passing the hat at our meetings wasn't enough. Prisoners must buy everything they want or need at the Commissary: shampoo, aspirin, tampax or pads, dental floss and more. Care packages were not allowed at most prisons. Stamps and phone calls were also a personal cost. The ability to stay in touch with friends and family was limited by how much money a prisoner had available. We wrote to everyone. Not all twenty-five felt they needed the money, but twelve women responded positively.

The political prisoners included women from many different movements. Debbie Sims Africa, Janet Holloway Africa, and Janine Phillips Africa were in the Black liberation group MOVE. Alejandrina Torres, Dylcia Pagán, Alicia Rodríguez Vélez, and Carmen Valentín were Puerto Rican Independentistas who served time for seditious conspiracy to overthrow the government. Norma Jean Croy was Native American. Marilyn Buck and Linda Evans were both North American anti-imperialists imprisoned for armed actions in support of revolution and Black liberation, Sara Jane Olson was in the Symbionese Liberation Army in the 1970s, and Helen Woodson served time for antinuclear activities. The primary source of income for this fund was Sparks Fly, a cultural/educational event in the fall that celebrated the International Day of Solidarity with Women Political Prisoners. For years, we also held huge garage sales in the Castro neighborhood to raise money. Out of Control and LAGAI were able to send money monthly for many years. It was important to us that all the prisoners knew the money was primarily donated from queer people in our community. As some women were paroled, the number shrank, and by 2006, money was being sent to six women.

Sparks Fly originated in 1989 as an International Day of Solidarity with Women Political Prisoners, and to commemorate the escape of Assata Shakur from prison. The event was organized by a coalition of groups including Out of Control, LAGAI, and Women Against Imperialism. In 1990, we named the annual event "Sparks Fly" after the poem by Susan Rosenberg.

Left to right, standing: Bo brown, Buss, Jane Segal, Mo Kalman; sitting: Jay Mullins; at Gay Pride 1988. The "Dykes Out of Control" T-shirts were a big hit.

Photo Credit: Unknown
Courtesy Out of Control Collection

The first year we raised $400 for the Commissary Fund, and in the fourteenth year we were able to send out over $4,000. Sparks Fly always featured speakers as well as music and comedy. There were local performers, writers, and poets, all donating their time, including Gwen Avery, Mary Watkins, Jewelle Gomez, and Chrystos. When we could afford it, we invited and flew people from across the country. Speakers might be former prisoners or members of other groups. Speakers represented important current struggles that were linked to ours. For example, Vieques, an island municipality of Puerto Rico, is known internationally as the site of a series of protests against the US Navy's use of the island as a bombing range and testing ground, which led to the Navy's departure in 2003. In 2002, a woman from the Committe for the Rescue and Development of Vieques spoke at Sparks Fly, and another year, letters were read aloud from some of the women still imprisoned. In 1999, Sparks Fly celebrated the release from prison of eleven Puerto Rican Nationalists, the return of Silvia Baraldini to Italy, and the release of Laura Whitehorn. In 2003, Sparks Fly 13 was honored to have as special guests Yuri Kochiyama, longtime activist and comrade of Malcolm X, and Lynne Stewart, NYC human rights attorney who later went to prison herself.

Sparks Fly 2010 honored Marilyn Buck and all women political prisoners. This was the last formal event called Sparks Fly.

Eleanor, a ninth grader and the daughter of an OOC member, opened Sparks Fly 11 with this statement: "I got involved with

Sparks Fly because I wanted to be part of a group that gives the women political prisoners money for stuff they don't get from the prisons—you know, extravagant luxuries like soap, toothpaste, toothbrushes, towels, sneakers. Should these women be forced to live under inhumane conditions simply because they were trying to make things better for all of us? Should any human be treated this way? I think not. But just thinking isn't going to change anything. I'm here and doing this because I want all of my friends to know about women political prisoners, and some of them have come tonight. Please tell your friends, too!"

The final issue of *Out of Time* was printed in 2013, and the last Sparks Fly was in 2010. Most of the women political prisoners we worked with have been released, and some have died. Some of us continue to do prisoner support work, and all of us are community activists. Prisons are still really awful, and the US still has the largest prison population in the world. The private for-profit prison industry based in the US is a multi-billion-dollar industry and is growing stronger by the minute. But the prison abolition movement is growing also. And there are still many groups working to close prisons in the US and support the people caught up in the criminal in-justice system.

OUT OF CONTROL MADE A DIFFERENCE
Susan Rosenberg

Out of Control made a difference. OOC's solidarity penetrated the solid steel, concrete walls, and razor wire, flowing through and into the bowels of the experimental women's high-security unit in the basement at Lexington, Kentucky, Federal Prison for Women. OOC formed to shut down the Lexington Control Unit and support women political prisoners and, in so doing, more than fortified our resistance for the two years of torture and isolation we experienced there. Solidarity matters.

The purpose of that early program of long-term solitary confinement and social isolation was to break us, to pressure us into renouncing our political beliefs. It was explicit: "Betray your politics and we will stop torturing you." The idea of extreme punishment is now standard American practice, and its intent is to strip the individual of their meaning, purpose, and identity.

The fact that some of us, myself included, were lesbians—and that we identified as revolutionary, anti-imperialist lesbians—put us under particular assault by the Bureau of Prisons jailers. So the idea that a group of lesbians, some of whom were our friends, comrades, and sisters, had formed to stop our torture and support who we actually were poured strength into us, into me. Knowing of the existence of OOC was a thread of a psychological, psychic, and literal lifeline. If OOC could be out of control, then it reminded me that I could be out of control.

OOC collaborated with others from the Puerto Rican independence movement, from the anti-imperialist left, from the prison movement, from the legal progressive and human rights communities, to shut down Lexington. At that time there were not that many openly lesbian organizations, and they were out and proud and fought the homophobia of all the movements by their very definition and their work.

What was so very important about OOC's solidarity was that they fought for our human rights and an end to extreme punishment, *and* they supported us because we were women political prisoners—we were from and of their movement. That was not easy to do. Our actions had left a wake of terrible state repression, and there were divisions in the left over our politics and choices. We were each convicted of the most serious charges, and all with lengthy sentences. For Alejandrina Torres, Puerto Rican prisoner of war, it was sedition; for Silvia Baraldini, it was conspiracy to support the Black Liberation Army and for helping to free Assata Shakur; for me, it was possession of weapons and associations with the Black Liberation Army and the Fuerzas Armadas de Liberación Nacional. While OOC did not necessarily support all our specific decisions, they did not bow to pressure to eliminate our political stand.

Susan Rosenberg while incarcerated.

Photo credit: Prison photo
Courtesy Out of Control Collection

Left to right: Stella the dog, Susan Rosenberg, and Dawn Reel in their home in Brooklyn, New York. 2021.

Where it was our political identities that were under attack, that kind of support was most crucial.

When we won the closing of the High Security Unit at Lexington, OOC continued their support of all of us. They made sacrifices to support us as we were sent to different prisons around the country. They visited us, they sent us money, and they traveled to other cities and joined our legal and popular defense work. After Lexington was shut down, they inspired and mobilized women and lesbians around the country to create other prisoner-support groups. They supported each and every one of us until we were released.

While we were political prisoners from a different time, an earlier time that was defined by the conditions of that time, the same can be said about the movements and support of that time. There are principles and commitments that OOC fought for that hold some lessons for us now. In the movements that work to reform and to abolish prisons, fighting for the lives of women and LGBTQ prisoners cannot be minimized simply because the numbers of women and LGBTQ people in the system are fewer than men. In fact, it's the opposite: we must put the most marginalized, the most oppressed, first. In so doing, we challenge the fundamental nature of the system and expose its utterly racist, misogynist, and repressive nature.

Solitary confinement is torture, and OOC helped all of us to understand that. OOC made solidarity material and active. They put their bodies on the line for those of us inside. As the still-held political prisoners from that era and the newest ones languish and die in prison, the need to free them becomes all the more imperative. While there are no easy answers, it takes our heart and soul to work for that freedom, and to fight for it as if they are us—as OOC did for us.

I did not thank them enough, but I thank them, I thank you all, now. OOC made a difference.

Susan Rosenberg
Former US political prisoner

OUT OF TIME

Issue No. 28 Out of Control--Lesbian Brunch Club to Support Women Political Prisoners June 1995

If you don't already, then...
WE WANT YOU TO KNOW: DYKE POLITICAL PRISONERS

LINDA EVANS

Linda is an out lesbian who has been committed to political action since 1967. She is currently serving a 38 year sentence for harboring a fugitive (3 years); possession of a weapon by a felon (2 years); false statements to acquire four legal guns and amunition (30 years) and convicted of "conspiracy to influence, change, and protest policies and practices of the US government concerning various international and domestic matters through the use of violent and illegal means" (5 years the Resistance Conspiracy Case).

In 1969 Linda participated in an anti-war delegation to North Vietnam to receive US-POW's released by the Vietnamese. While living in Austin, Texas Linda was a political/cultural worker active in the women's movement and the lesbian community; street theater, a women's band and a women's printing/graphics collective. She also organized support for struggles led by Black and Chicano/Mexicano grassroots organizations against the KKK, forced sterilization and killer cops. Her solidarity work was international as well: Southern Africa, Palestine, and Central America. Linda is currently incarcerated at FCI Dublin, CA. She is an artist, attending New College thru the mail and an AIDS activist inside. **Linda Evans#19973-054 5701 8th Street, Camp Parks Dublin, CA 94568**

cont'd next page Out of Time

SUSAN ROSENBERG

Susan is an out lesbian and has been a political activist all of her adult life. She is currently serving a sentence of 58 years for 8 counts possession of weapons, explosives , and identifications. Susan's sentence is the longest ever received for a possessory offense.

In high school Susan worked with the Young Lords Party and the Black Panther Party. She was active in the anti-Vietnam war and women's movements. In the 1970's she worked in support of the Puerto Rican Independence Movement and the Black Liberation struggle. She is a Doctor of Acupuncture who studied at the Black Acupuncture Advisory Association of

cont'd next page Out of Time

Out of Time
c/o Out of Control Lesbian Committee
3543—18th Street, Box 30
San Francisco, CA 94110

Laura Whitehorn

I am serving a 23-year sentence for revolutionary activities including what the government called "conspiracy to oppose, protest, and change the policies and practices of the united states government in domestic and international matters by violence and illegal means."

I was one of seven anti-imperialists charged in the Resistance and Conspiracy case. Throughout my political life, I've supported the right to human rights and self determination of Third World struggles around the world and inside the united states.

The actions for which I am imprisoned were one small attempt in a long term effort to build a revolutionary solidarity movement capable of struggling on a lot of levels.

Since my arrest in Baltimore in 1985, I've experienced first hand how the government treats political prisoners: held for over three years in "preventative detention" (no bail), kept in solitary confinement for much of the time, classified as a "special handling/high security" prisoner because of my political beliefs and associations.

In prison I've been involved in work to educate prisoners about HIV and Aids, and to develop support for people with

cont'd next page Out of Time

Norma Jean Croy

In 1978, Norma Jean, her brother Patrick Hooty Croy, and three other relatives, stopped at a convenience store before going to their Grandfather's cabin to go hunting. Following an altercation initiated by the store clerk, local police chased Norma Jean and the others as they headed out of town. When they arrived at their Grandfather's cabin, the police drove up and began chasing them. The police fired shots, hitting her cousin as he stood up to surrender, and Norma in the back. Norma's brother, Hooty, was also shot in the back twice before he turned around and fired one shot, which struck an officer in the heart.

In 1979, Norma Jean and her companions were charged with first-degree murder of a police officer which typically carries a much higher sentence than first-degree murder of a civilian. Norma and her brother were convicted, even though there was no evidence that Norma Jean fired any weapon. Hooty was sentenced to death; Norma Jean was given life in prison.

In 1985, Hooty's conviction was reversed by the California Supreme Court. Norma Jean's appeal was denied by a lower court. In his 1990 retrial, Hooty was acquitted of the murder and related charges on the grounds of self-defense. The trial judge stated, "...had Norma Jean Croy been tried in the case I heard, she would have been found not guilty."

ACTION ALERT! GOV. SIGNS MUMIA'S DEATH WARRANT
The Penn. Governor has signed Mumia's execution for August 21, 1995. There are currently demonstrations nationwide, and an urgent phone and fax zap to Judge Sabo (215) 686-5100 and fax (215) 563-1623.
On JUNE 25 AT 7:30 PM AT MARTIN LUTHER KING JR, JUNIOR HIGH SCHOOL IN BERKELEY Mumia's son, and his attorney will be there. Adrienne Rich, Michael Parenti, Piri Thomas, Chrystos and Judi Bari will read from *Live From Death Row*. Proceeds from all readings will benefit Mumia's legal fund at the Black United Fund in Philadelphia. For info call (510) 848-6767.

Out of Time exposed readers to the presence of women inside US prisons. This issue headlines four dyke political prisoners. Elevating the visibility of lesbians and women political prisoners was central to Out of Control's work. *Out of Time* included women who kill in self-defense, LGBT cases, and the enormous growth of the US prison industrial complex.

INTERVIEW WITH JUDITH MIRKINSON (MIRK)
Brooke Lober

Mirk: The four of us sat around in Jane Segal's kitchen, at her kitchen table. It was me, Jane Segal, Jay Mullins, and bo brown. And we said, "We have to do something."

Jane and I had known Silvia for a long time. Jane knew her in college, and I knew her since 1970. And then bo and Jay met her later, and visited her when she was in FCI Dublin. So we said, "Okay, we have to do something." And we started forming a committee about it. I forget, we had some very long name, which Jane remembers, like the Women's Committee to Free Political Prisoners from Isolation . . . Something along those lines. She'll remember.

So we started doing work, and then in '87, there were other people beginning to do work, too. The Puerto Ricans were doing work around Alejandrina Torres, because Alejandrina and Susan Rosenberg got moved there next.

And really, the Lexington Control Unit was made for them. It was an experiment, and they moved two other people in there also so they could claim that it wasn't for political prisoners, but it was. It was the first isolation unit, and maximum-security unit of that sort, for women. There had previously been one at Alderson; Lolita Lebrón had been there with bo, actually. But it wasn't the same. Lexington was all white, it was in a basement, and there were only five people there. They were under constant surveillance, even in the shower. They gave them TVs, to be nice, but other than that . . . It was blindingly white. I think they were modeling it after Stammheim, which had been the prison that the RAF [Red Army Faction] prisoners had been in.

It wasn't quite as stark as that, but it was that model. I mean, now there are tons of them for women. Carswell, there's one, and

. . . of course there are many for men. But Lexington at that time was the first one [for women]. And really, the purpose of Lexington was to break them. Their whole thing, and still to this day, was: you have to recant, and you have to say you're sorry, and you have to say, "Everything I did was wrong."

Left to right: Susan Rosenberg and Judith Mirkinson (Mirk), DC jail, circa 1990. Susan Rosenberg and six other defendants awaited trial as part of the Resistance Conspiracy case. In 1990 Mirk and a team of activists went to the DC jail to interview the defendants for a documentary produced by Lisa Rudman. This photo was taken during the production.

You have to say, "The worst thing that can possible happen to you is to go to prison, and nobody should follow our example." It was very, very hard for them. So there began to be this campaign by the Puerto Ricans, by the World Council of Churches and other church groups, and we joined that effort out here.

There were people already doing work around the Marion control unit, but this was very specifically about women, and so we joined it. We had done work around Marion and elsewhere; we'd all been doing work around political prisoners, anyway. But this was very specific.

We had all been visiting, out at Dublin, the Puerto Rican prisoners of war, and we had visited Silvia there, and Laura Whitehorn . . . I can't remember whether she was there yet; I don't think so. We decided that we had to do something. We decided that we wanted to do a demonstration at Dublin, which was called Pleasanton.

So we gathered a bunch of women that we knew—mostly from the lesbian community, but also other women—and we formed this group. Mostly we formed it in my living room, and it was a very interesting process, because there were all these different personalities [laughs] and different political tendencies. In those days, you could have been two degrees different and it was a big deal.

TEAR DOWN THE WALL!!
NO POLITICAL SHOW TRIAL
SUPPORT THE RESISTANCE CONSPIRACY 6!!

Sticker Credit: unknown
Courtesy Out of Control Collection

This is one of many ways activists spread the word about the "Resistance Conspiracy 6."

But we did it: we worked together, and we wrote pamphlets; we demonstrated; people went to Gay Day and passed out fliers there. And we did all this work around the Lexington Control Unit. We learned a lot, because eventually Amnesty [International] actually joined the campaign, and one thing that they taught us is that you can't be a human being, have human interaction, unless you're with thirty-five people. You can't have too many people, and you can't have too few people. You have to have interactions to actually have good mental health. And these five women, while they were allowed some visitors (on a very restricted list) for the most part all they ever saw were guards. Also, you can't be in an atmosphere that is just monochromatic, especially white. It's a form of torture, actually, after a while.

There was a huge amount of pressure put on the prison. So you know what they decided to do? They decided that they would paint half the wall beige [laughs]. And they also said, "Okay, we'll give them curtains in the showers." That was their big compromise. So that's how the campaign got started.

At Out of Control's meetings and events, on the one hand, everybody was arguing all the time. But they were also great, because it was this group of women who really liked each other, despite whatever personality differences we had. We basically had political unity; we were very concerned about our friends in the control unit, and we were really determined that we were gonna do something and get them out. So I think all those things were really positive, and Out of Control then grew and developed around the whole issue of political prisoners.

Brooke: Why do you think it's important, or why do you think it happened, that a group worked on the issue of women political prisoners specifically?

Mirk: We were anti-imperialists, so we had a very broad view of the world. We considered these women our comrades, our sisters; we felt, also, that often women are left out of the equation, and it's still true that men get much more attention than women do.

It was part of our feminism, actually, that we combined our anti-imperialism, our anti–US empire, our antirepression, all into one package. And we felt, also, that we could reach out to women everywhere about this and educate them. But we weren't just educating them about women; we were also educating them about the nature of the prison system, and the nature of political repression. And I think that was a very, very valuable lesson.

BO BROWN, THE GENTLEMAN BANK ROBBER
Julie Perini

Bo's rich and varied community, which included former members of Out of Control, organized a benefit for bo brown in 2017.

"I am an anti-authoritarian lesbian feminist anarcho-communist. I am an urban guerrilla committed to give my white life if necessary." —bo brown, February 21, 1978

Bo brown read this statement on February 21, 1978, at the federal courthouse in Portland, Oregon. The judge sentenced her to twenty-five years in prison on federal bank robbery and firearms charges for actions carried out with the George Jackson Brigade. She served eight years, but she never stopped being a revolutionary freedom fighter.

I first met bo brown in 2012 at a bar after a prison abolition conference in Portland. She was holding court with several young radicals. I assumed she was imparting knowledge, strategies, advice. As I neared the conversation, I quickly learned she was instead singing the many praises of Bisquick, a premixed baking mixture well-suited for biscuits, pancakes, and oh, so much more. I immediately felt at ease and at home in the presence of this warm, wise soul.

Photo credit: Unknown
Courtesy Etang Inyang

Rita bo brown circa 1986, in San Francisco, after she was paroled.

Soon afterward, organizer Lydia Bartholow and I hatched a plan to interview bo, to get her life story on tape, in her own words. We did not know that this initial idea would lead to *The Gentleman Bank Robber: The Life Story of Butch Lesbian Freedom Fighter rita bo brown*, a 46- minute documentary film that includes interviews with bo, her friends, her comrades, and community members. The film weaves together personal and political perspectives on twentieth-century social movement histories, including queer liberation in the 1960s; militant underground activity with the George

Jackson Brigade, a revolutionary group, in the 1970s; political prisoner–support work in the 1980s; and prison-activist work into the present day. *The Gentleman Bank Robber* has screened all over the world since its release in 2017, often presented by feminist, queer, and anarchist community groups.

Rita "bo" brown was born in 1947 in Klamath Falls in southern Oregon. As the daughter of a working-poor coal-mining family, she experienced many challenges against this rural backdrop. Rigid gender, race, and class positions were maintained through schools and other institutions. She moved to Salem and eventually Seattle, where she found welcoming queer communities that encouraged her to be who she really was: a butch lesbian. She worked at the post office, one of the few employers that allowed her to wear pants to work. Pilfering $50 from the post office in order to make ends meet landed her her first of two prison sentences in 1971—a judgment that had more to do with her refusal to conform to gender norms than her need for rehabilitation.

In prison, bo encountered Black women with a high level of political consciousness who shared books and political analysis with her. By the time bo returned to life on the outside, she had a new understanding of systemic oppression and the role prisons play in it. She joined with other politically active formerly incarcerated people to organize support for people behind bars. In 1975, bo joined several other ex-prisoners in the George Jackson Brigade, a group of seven associates in the Pacific Northwest, living underground under assumed identities, carrying out militant direct actions in Oregon and Washington in solidarity with peace movements, labor unions, Black liberation, and other struggles at the time. After a massive search by the FBI, all of the Brigade members were caught and many were incarcerated, some for several decades. Bo served time in federal prisons from 1978 through 1986. She was incarcerated alongside Black Liberation Army member Assata Shakur, and the two became friends. Upon her release, she moved to San Francisco, where she cofounded the Out of Control: Lesbian Committee to Support Women Political Prisoners. They worked to shut down the notorious maximum-security unit in Lexington, Kentucky, that housed four women: two anti-imperialist political prisoners, one Puerto Rican prisoner of war, and one "social prisoner".

My collaborators, Lydia Bartholow and Erin McNamara, interviewed bo and her comrades and friends over several years in Oakland, California, where bo now lives[1], and Portland, Oregon, where I live. Bo and her partner e-tang generously shared their home with us. I will never forget staying up late into the night, talking with bo about her extraordinary life, sorting through her personal archive of letters she received while in prison, her FBI file, and other social-movement ephemera. These are the stories that need to be preserved and told to future generations: stories of people who have the vision to see a liberated world and the strength to demand it.

In closing, let me share just a few of the many gems we received from our interviews with bo:

What was robbing a bank like?

"I practiced and practiced and practiced and practiced in the mirror and everything else, till I went in the bank and said to the lady, 'This is a robbery. Put the money in the bag.' . . . I never had to take my gun out. I always just had it here, in my pants. They always thought I was a man. I was always polite. I said 'please, thank you, I don't want this to last any longer than you do.'"

What was the hardest part of being underground?

"Not being able to go to a gay bar. Not being around other gay people. Not seeing other lesbians. I came out of a very strong lesbian community. I had to not be who I was. I had to be 'John's sister.' I couldn't be me."

What are your thoughts on violent direct action?

---

[1] this essay was written before bo brown passed away in October, 2021

"When you take stuff to that level, it opens up a different avenue, a way to communicate to the public. You use sensationalism as a way of expression; it's a different tool."

How do you feel about your actions with the Brigade now that you're older?

"I'm not sorry I did that. At all. That's what I thought I needed to do and that's what I did. And I think I did it honorably and honestly, and I didn't hurt anybody. And I think that our whole point was to make people pay attention to other things in life, and I think they did that."

Why did you cofound Out of Control: Lesbian Committee to Support Women Political Prisoners?

"There ARE women political prisoners. And that was the focus. No one else was doing any work around women political prisoners. Just like there's no one doing any work around women political prisoners now."

Clockwise from top left: Rita bo brown at her sentencing, US District Court in Portland, Oregon, February 21, 1978. Rita bo brown reading *Out of Time*, San Francisco, August 2012. Rita bo brown outside her house on her truck, Oakland, California, August 2012. Drawing of rita bo brown with other revolutionaries, artist and date unknown. Rita bo brown, Gay Olympics, San Francisco, California, circa 1988.

LIFE IS LIVING

Annie Danger

"Struggle is good and change is good. They are not easy, but isn't that what life is?

Is life really about making it easy so you can sit on your ass all the time and not do a motherfucking thing?

I don't think so. I think life is living.

"I sat down to draw bo how I see her, frank and ready And still with a spark or three. I had planned to do a Study, then rework it into a more careful line drawing, but This first shot came out so lovely, so bo, there was Nothing left to do. Rough edges, rock solid center, quite a few sparks. <3.

INTERVIEW WITH JANE SEGAL

Brooke Lober

Brooke: How did you get started as a political activist, before Out of Control?

Jane: I was very active in SDS [Students for a Democratic Society] when I went to college in Madison, Wisconsin. Then in 1970, I moved to Portland, Oregon, where I was involved in antiwar activity. I moved with a women's collective from Madison to Portland, and we were gonna do political work. That didn't materialize the way that we, as a collective, wanted it to, but we lived collectively, supported each other's politics, and did work that was primarily about the [Vietnam] war and women's health. I went through many deep personal changes when I lived in Portland. Soon after moving, I came out as a lesbian, which was life-changing for me. And I lived in the Portland dyke community that was developing, and pretty much exploding, by the mid-, late '70s. Women's liberation and gay liberation were happening big time, and we were part of it all.

In Portland I worked in a federally funded daycare center for years, and my feeling was that I really wanted to bring my student and intellectual politics into the grassroots, and to bring it down home. I was part of the student movement in Madison, and that was grassroots; it was not just armchair intellectualism. But now I wanted to be an activist in the community, in social services, more than speaking about political stuff, more than being a movement organizer.

I was an SDS organizer in Madison. We traveled around the state talking about the war in Vietnam and the Black Panthers. The group I was a part of had a relationship with the Black Panther Party, and with chairman Fred Hampton in Chicago. I was very aware of national liberation struggles within this country, and not just internationally. I supported self-determination for Black people and Brown people.

So, when I moved to California from Portland, because of my consciousness, I started doing solidarity work. I was committed to antiracist politics, so I tried to work with several groups in the Bay Area. One was the John Brown Anti-Klan Committee, and then after that I tried with a women's committee that was around Central America, and I don't remember the name of it. It was solidarity work but, for one reason or another, it wasn't a good fit for me.

Out of Control was really my political work for a very long time. My deep involvement with Out of Control led me to participate in a lot of activities and a lot of campaigns for women political prisoners and Puerto Rican prisoners of war. But we didn't come to it just because of the Lexington High Security Unit—I mean, yes, we came to it in response to the opening of Lexington, the high-security, subterranean, small-group isolation, experimental control unit for women political prisoners and one prisoner of war.

Earlier on there was a high-security control unit for women within FCI Alderson, West Virginia. Bo was there, and so was Assata Shakur. Both of these units were explicitly political because they were locking up women political prisoners and Puerto Rican POWs. But the control unit at Lexington was more specific, very brutal, and very horrible. I visited Silvia at Lexington, and it was intense.

I came to Out of Control with a lot of political organizing behind me. And bo did too. And Mirk did too. And Jay did too. So I would say that the four of us who founded Out of Control had the politics of the time, of the late '60s and the '70s. We formed the group in '87, but we were formed earlier on. Bo and I are the same age. Mirk and Jay are a little younger.

Our first action was a demo against the Lexington Control Unit, in January of '87. And we kept going. By '98, it was the Critical Resistance (CR) conference. We were involved in the organizing of CR; Bo and I were on the organizing committee for the conference. So that's about eleven years. And during that time, we were doing a lot of educational work and agitation. First around Lexington, and then when Lexington closed, we were doing work around women political prisoners and Puerto Rican women prisoners of war. Our focus was the women political prisoners and POWs. There were so many of them; we needed to make sure they weren't forgotten. We wanted the women to be visible.

THERE ARE WOMEN POLITICAL PRISONERS IN U.S.

A political prisoner is anyone jailed because of their self-conscious political actions against the government. We believe that all prisoners are political because the laws and the courts in this country are completely political and not at all fair.

Womyn have been imprisoned for the following political acts:
- providing sanctuary for Central American refugees
- anti-nuclear and anti-military activities
- self defense against sexual abuse
- fighting for Black liberation
- defending land and treaty rights of Native peoples
- refusing to testify before a grand jury in a government investigation
- fighting for the independence of Puerto Rico from the U.S.
- defending the rights of lesbians and gay men

There are over 100 political prisoners and Prisoners of War in the U.S. now, at least 25% of them wimmin.

Susan   Alejandrina   Silvia

In October 1986 the Federal Bureau of Prisons opened a new control unit specifically for wymyn political prisoners. Currently incarcerated are:

- Alejandrina Torres: Active in Chicago's Puerto Rican community through her church as well as an alternative high school and clinic. When arrested in 1983 she assumed Prisoner of War status. Serving 35 years for seditious conspiracy.

- Susan Rosenberg: A Northamerican political prisoner who has worked in solidarity with the New Afrikan and Puerto Rican movements. She's dedicated her life to anti-imperialist struggles. Sentenced to 58 years for possession of weapons, explosives and false I.D..

- Silvia Baraldini: An anti-imperialist Northamerican who has worked for years in solidarity with the New Afrikan Independence Movement. She comes from an Italian family long involved in the resistance against fascism. She is serving 43 years for charges of conspiracy (under RICO) stemming from Grand Juries called to investigate the 1981 Brinks case.

Design Credit: Out of Control — Courtesy Out of Control Collection

Out of Control produced this flyer during the National Campaign to Shut Down the Lexington HSU. This flyer moves beyond Lexington politically and lists women imprisoned for a wide range of actions, including self-defense against sexual abuse. Out of Control often used the slogan "There Are Women Political Prisoners In US;" used the slogan, to expose the reality of women incarcerated in the US for their political thoughts and actions.

At the beginning, we did guerilla theater about the High Security Unit at Lexington at Gay Pride and other places. We made "Dykes Out of Control, Shut Down Lexington Control Unit" T-shirts that we sold at Pride. We did major events; we also made T-shirts that said "Dykes from Hell." We did the T-shirts with LAGAI, and we always shared a PRIDE table with LAGAI. We worked a lot with LAGAI: Lesbians and Gays Against Intervention, and they had a newsletter called *UltraViolet*. A few years after we started our group, we started publishing our newsletter *Out Of Time*, which was inside *UltraViolet* until 2013. So that's a long time, and we had a close relationship with LAGAI.

Norma Jean Croy, Silvia Baraldini, the Puerto Ricans, the Resistance Conspiracy defendants: we worked on all their campaigns a lot. Marilyn "Mo" Kalman moved to Washington, DC, for a number of months to work on the Resistance Conspiracy case. They did note cards to raise money, and they did a booklet of poetry. We were an informal West Coast distribution for both of those projects.

So we had our newsletter, and we had an educational/cultural event, Sparks Fly, and we did a major garage sale. The garage sale and Sparks Fly raised money for the Women Political Prisoner Commissary Fund. Lots of people came to Sparks Fly. It was a big event, and we did that in collaboration with other groups. We didn't do that alone. LAGAI, individual women, and Women Against Imperialism worked on Sparks Fly. The garage sale was an event that was organized and staffed by just LAGAI and us.

The commissary fund was another collaboration between OOC and LAGAI. We raised money for commissary for the women political prisoners and the Puerto Rican POWs who were inside. We were trying to break down the prison walls, break down the isolation of the women inside with support and communication.

This was the point of our newsletter: to give people on the outside real information about what was going on inside. And to give people inside information about other people who were inside—and the movement outside. That was our strategy; that was a big objective for us. What else: raise money for commissary and educate. But we didn't say, "What's our strategy?" We didn't discuss our work in those terms. We planned, we acted, followed through, and just kind of evolved. We were not a Marxist-Leninist organization. We didn't define ourselves in that way. We were a collective, a group of antiracist, feminist, anti-homophobic dykes.

Brooke: Did people ask, "Why are lesbians working for political prisoners?"

Left to right: Jane Segal, Dylcia Pagán, and rita bo brown. This celebration took place in the Bay Area, September 1999, when the Puerto Rican Independentistas were released from prison.

Jane: Well, yes. I felt like we initially got involved, the group of us that initiated this project that became Out of Control, because we knew many of the women personally who became political prisoners. We all knew Silvia Baraldini when she was transferred from FCI Dublin to the HSU, Lexington. We viewed ourselves as being in the same movement that they were in; we just weren't doing what they were doing. So it was about solidarity, and it was about "all of us or none," in that broad sense of the term: that we are here to protect those locked up that are our political sisters—political comrades who have done this work. We didn't launch an armed struggle/nonarmed struggle argument there. It wasn't about, "Do you support what these people did?" We didn't really get into what happened. We supported them.

The way we tried to get at it was support for their politics. The women we were supporting inside were anti-imperialist, and they were anticapitalist, and they were pro–National Liberation struggle, and they were totally pro–LGBT rights and –women's rights. They were feminists. We were feminists. I am a feminist. Absolutely. It's just, Out of Control was more than feminist—I mean, we tried to educate in the women's community and in the gay and lesbian community, but the way that it wound up, the way it worked out, it was lesbians who were running it and doing it and working in it for the longest period of time, and who were still doing it at the end. We were a lesbian group.

INTERVIEW WITH JENNIFER BEACH
Brooke Lober

Brooke: Can you tell me how you got into Out of Control?

Jennifer: Sure. That name, "Out of Control," was really important—that we were women, or lesbians, or dykes Out of Control. We were not going to be under control. And we were against control units, because they are particularly visible orchestrations of state control over women's lives. That was, in some ways, maybe the dominant politic. And it was international in its analysis.

I was not there at the formation, but I was there pretty soon after. I think it was 1986. I was nineteen years old, and I took a class at San Francisco State that was cotaught by Chinosole and Angela Davis on women; it was called Incarcerated Women. They had several speakers come, and simultaneously, I was going to a lot of events. I was part of the women's movement. I was part of the left, a little bit, but just a little tiny bit, because I didn't know that many people.

Bo brown came and spoke in the class and through that, I found out about this demonstration, about the Lexington Control Unit. Then I went to the demonstration, and then either Jane Segal or Leslie Mullin invited me to come to a meeting, an Out of Control meeting. That's kinda how I remember the story.

I was very young. And it turns out that I lived a block away from bo brown. This was the great thing about the Mission in those days: it was a place for people outside of the mainstream of the world. So we ended up in the same place. Bo brown was a former political prisoner who had very recently gotten out of prison, and I was a nineteen-year-old whose father had recently died and who was opening up to a whole world.

Bo and I made this big connection. We were understanding the world together. Even though we're completely different—from completely different backgrounds and had different styles—we made this big connection. She really was . . . I wouldn't say that Out of Control was formed by bo's spirit, but for sure, it was one of the big informing cultural aspects of Out of Control.

Jane Segal and Jennifer Beach at Gay Pride, circa 1988. Out of Control and LAGAI (Lesbians and Gays Against Intervention) did outreach and tabling at Gay Pride, increasing the visibility of women political prisoners in the LGBTQ community.

Brooke: Can you say more about that? The cultural aspects of Out of Control?

Jennifer: Well, bo brown is a working-class woman who's very butch, who was in the George Jackson Brigade. If you walked into a meeting, there would be bo, with a big beard, big woman, big butch woman, bearded lady, leaning back in a chair, and saying kind of wildly militant things. For me—I'm sure other people have different reactions—it made me feel super comfortable, like you could be anything here in this room. And because I knew her outside, we had a particularly sweet, warm kind of thing.

And Jane Segal is an artist. The first project we did together, that I remember, was working on this street theater about the

Lexington Control Unit. She and I sat down, and we invited Camo from Prairie Fire to help us make this tape of strange music to add to the street theater piece. There was a kind of artistic element in Out of Control that seemed a little more anarchistic or open. In Out of Control, you could join a project even it was kind of outside of your knowledge. I'd never worked on any kind of music tape before. It was loose, in that sense. Out of Control had a narrow focus, and that allowed people to be a little bit broader in their conversations.

Brooke: Why do you think it was important to focus on women political prisoners?

Jennifer: Out of Control was really originally formed to combat the Lexington Control Unit, which did target women political prisoners. And Out of Control felt that that was not a coincidence—that they started with women in what seemed pretty clearly to be a direction that that [the Federal Bureau of Prisons] was going to go in, in terms of what was borrowed from the German model of managing political prisoners. And there's some things in the report about the severity of the conditions. It was painted all white, and in many ways it replicated conditions in mental institutions, where women had also been placed when they were "unruly".

That analysis—that there are particular ways the state tries to control women and uses women as guinea pigs—I associate that analysis with Out of Control. This was an experimental unit, Lexington, and they chose women political prisoners first. So we saw that as an expression of the misogyny of the state. We felt that there were particular challenges faced by women in prison, and there were particular challenges faced by women political prisoners; we wanted to, in our small way, focus on that experience and that repression, in collaboration with these larger movements, like the Puerto Rican independence movement. Across the country there were a lot of organizations that were focusing on prisoners and political prisoners. We did not see ourselves as divorced from them, but felt that we were going to have this focus on the experience of women.

When Critical Resistance started ten years later, they said they were going to foreground the experience of women, but not focus on it. So that was a different frame, which I think had a lot of power and actually incorporated some of the same elements of being open, not restrictive, but having a focus.

Critical Resistance went on to do other things later, but in the original meetings about the conference that was what was said. They said, and people were very clear, "This is how we see it. We see the conference, before it was an organization, as foregrounding the experience of women. But not having an exclusive focus on it." And you see that same approach in Ellen Barry's organization, Legal Services for Prisoners with Children. For some people, the first kinds of people they think of when they hear "Prisoners with Children" are mothers and women. But that's not accurate, right? So Ellen Barry tried to hold that multiplicity of experience in the name of the organization.

That same awareness of gender difference, without an exclusive focus on women, was true for Critical Resistance, at least in the beginning. I can't really speak to the evolution of that process later. But for Out of Control, it was both similar to those groups and also different in its focus. We were not trying to be a mass national project or a dominant voice in the national movement, and we were committed to highlighting the experience of women political prisoners, which no one else was exactly doing that way.

Brooke: In the literature about women political prisoners, the issue of sexual abuse comes up a lot. Do you remember discussions about that, or the focus on that?

Jennifer: Well, bo had done really hard time. Bo was in prison for eight years. She was part of the George Jackson Brigade in the Northwest, and they were convicted of a series of bank robberies of appropriations to support the Black Liberation movement. Bo was a very masculine-presenting woman and was moved a lot, and was sometimes placed in men's prisons, and was very informed by the trauma that came out of that whole experience.

So that was something that was present in every meeting that we had—that truth of her personal experience. And at Lexington, it was unavoidable, right? You just had these women who were being videotaped, in the shower, every minute of every experience they had. They were strip-searched going in and out of every visit—which now is much more commonplace than it was then. Now, that's pretty much a lot what happens, but then it wasn't as common.

And you couldn't step away from the predatory sexual nature of that: the way that the constant threat of sexual violence and sexual invasion impacted the experience, living day to day.

Brooke: Among groups that work on behalf of political prisoners, it probably was kind of rare that a feminist group would call attention to sexual violence, because even though men might experience sexual violence in different ways, or women had as well, that was often outside the discussion.

Jennifer: I do think that it was a good contribution to the conversation. I don't think that it was considered controversial or wrong to bring it up. . . . I have a pretty rosy lens, so I might be missing elements. I mean, for sure in different moments, we felt disrespected by other organizations, but I don't feel like anybody disagreed with that set of truths. No one said, "You shouldn't be doing this." I think we felt sometimes like people, some men in larger formations, would dismiss us on the basis of us being women but not because they disagreed with the points we were making. So it was more mundane, pedestrian, leftist sexism rather than a political difference.

Brooke: How much do you think the campaign work you all did appealed to the women's movement? Or how do you think it was seen?

Jennifer: Well, I'm gonna go one step back. I got my degree in what was then called "women's studies" at San Francisco

State in the late '80s. And that course that I just talked about—Incarcerated Women, that was taught by Chinosole and Angela Davis—had been taught in previous years by a white woman, about incarcerated women and a lot about mental institutions.

So, I feel like I came into the academic, or the more formally structured, women's movement at a time when the mainstream women's movement was examining racism in a different way. There were Angela Davis, Cherríe Moraga, Gloria Anzaldúa. The theory of feminism was becoming more explicitly antiracist. Even though I hate the term "white feminism," I think that feminism is a very complicated trajectory of thought, and I feel like when you say "white feminism" you're saying everything before now is assimilationist. And I think actually some of the best examples of antiracism you find among white people were in the women's community, so I prefer the term "liberal feminism" to indicate that kind of assimilationism. I am very critical of liberal feminism, but I don't like it when people use those terms interchangeably, because I feel like it obviates, it veils, a serious and long-standing antiracist tradition. And some of the best antiracist work that was done by white people was done by the women's movement.

For instance, we did this event, Sparks Fly, and we could always get A-list talent. Dorothy Allison was happy to come, to read. Jewelle Gomez. Melanie DeMore. People who normally would've been a little outside of our range, but they all came down for this. Then they brought their own people. I think we really saw ourselves trying to tap into cultural leadership in that way, and I think we were actually relatively effective given that it was all on a pretty small scale. People like Jewelle Gomez, Dorothy Allison, Chrystos—these, at the time, A-list cultural names within our circles—did understand about prisons. They did understand about disenfranchised voices, they did understand about women in prison, and they wanted to lend their support, and they wanted to bring their people to hear more about those things.

In that sense, I feel like Sparks Fly was much more important and powerful than I fully realized at the time. It was always exciting to be like, "Oh, Dorothy Allison is coming to our event?" This was shocking to me; she had won all these awards, and she is somewhat reclusive. Cherríe Moraga. These people participated. That element in a certain way was more successful in terms of trying to build a base consciousness than what we might think of as—"conventional" is the wrong word, but what we might think of as the women's community or the lesbian community.

Selisse Berry holding the Out of Control banner at an International Women's Day event. Selisse was a member of Women Against Imperialism. A poster of the political prisoner Linda Evans is visible in the background on the right side. Out of Control joined International Women's Day demonstrations and the Dyke March with their banner and photo posters of the women political prisoners and POWs.

Brooke: It sounds like the feminist movement, at least at the grassroots, really was "with" you at that time.

Jennifer: In some ways, yes. OOC focused on building support for political prisoners, but as individuals, we were all also part of a larger political movement that included many other issues and street demonstrations. Our analysis about political repression and intermovement conflict impacted our navigation of street demonstrations. For instance, in this period there were many demonstrations in which there was conflict between the "nonviolent" demonstrators and the "black bloc" demonstrators that was not resolved. That was a high point of tension and conflict, and part of why those of us who were bridging those worlds struggled so much was that we wanted to have a frank, honest, supportive relationship with the black bloc.

We were sometimes critical, but we refused to criminalize political prisoners or militant action. There were so many people in feminist movements who described themselves and their philosophies as "nonviolent." These were, and are, the people who saw explicitly nonviolent commitments as the only way to protest. They did participate in criminalizing political prisoners, and militant movements, in ways that we would never do—because at the end of the day, one of the things that always has to come up is the choice of some of these women political prisoners, whom we supported, to engage in armed struggle. For the mainstream left, that's been a source of contention. A big problem in terms of building support for the prisoners—for the women and for the men—was people who said, "I never thought you should do this in the first place." In OOC we probably all had our personal dividing line about what we might do, but we did not engage in criticizing tactics, which we saw as divisive and dangerous. Now we have a great clause that addresses many of these issues in a positive way: "We embrace a diversity of tactics." This gives space to negotiate differences respectfully. The movements of the '80s, '90s, and early 2000s were missing that important language.

From how I see it now, that was a conflict that we encountered. I felt like I never had that conversation with these "peace"-identified, women-identified lesbians. It didn't quite come up.

Even though obviously there's a big peacenik element to that community, it didn't come up explicitly very often.

We would start with more points of commonality, right? It's not like everybody loved it. We didn't talk that much about charges. "What was Susan Rosenberg convicted of?" That didn't exactly come up a lot in conversation, but it didn't matter.

"CHOWCHILLA: GATEWAY TO PROSPERITY"

Chrystos

There are over 2,000 roses
planted in a straight stern line
in front of the last row of barbed wire
around the prison
for the pleasure of the passersby
I am a gardener whose roses cost $10 a piece
at the discount store
The usual fee for landscaping labor is $15 an hour
The irrigation system through this hot dry country
cost a minimum of $5,000
Our taxes paid for these roses you might never see
The women locked inside Chowchilla
whom we have been brainwashed to fear
for their poverty or their race
or their drug addictions
or their love of a man the kops caught
are dying and in pain from lack of medical care
In California there are more prisons than any other state
Per capita, it imprisons more people than any other place worldwide
The cost of a college education there
has risen 500% in 5 years
This money is used for prisons
Once in the top 10 for universities
it now ranks 41
In a 2-square-mile area over 6,000 women
will be locked down with no doctor employed full-time
Health care costs each prisoner $5 per visit
with a guard trained in a first aid course
The strongest pain medication given
even for those dying of AIDS/SIDA

is Tylenol
Starting salary for a guard
the majority of whom are male
& often sexually abuse their powerless female prisoners
is $30,000 a year plus benefits
also paid for by our taxes
All prisoners are required to work
even those mentally ill
for wages as low as $6 a month
The roses & irrigation system could have paid
a year's salary for a woman doctor
Have I become a thorn in your side yet
or will you pass by the razor wire of these words
looking to smell the roses

First printed in *Out of Time* 30 (December 1995)

Photo Credit: Unknown
Courtesy: Out of Control Collection

Chrystos is a First Nations (Menominee) lesbian poet who participated in many Sparks Fly events. She also held writing workshops at FCI Dublin and met many of the women political prisoners and POWs.

SECTION 2: SOLIDARITY WITH THE PUERTO RICAN INDEPENDENCE MOVEMENT

INTERVIEW WITH FRANKIE FREE RAMOS
Brooke Lober

Brooke: Let's start just by asking you to tell us about your young life and your route into activism.

Frankie: Okay. I was born in Puerto Rico, and I moved back and forth a lot in my early years. My father's Puerto Rican but was born and raised in New York. I was born in Puerto Rico, but when I was little, we moved as a family to New York, and he was very abusive. So my mom, when she left him, went all the way to San Diego, where she had a half-brother that she barely knew. But that kind of violence in the home was just like my earliest memories and the first five years of my life.

Things would be hard with a single mom, and my brother was born *travieso*. There is not a good word for that in English. He was born into the madness, so it's also not his fault, but it would just get hard. And so we would move back to Puerto Rico, multiple times. We moved back to Puerto Rico where my grandparents could take care of me and my brother, and my mom could work in the San Juan area, but she was always drawn back to San Diego. So we'd go back to San Diego.

When I was about maybe sixteen, my brother started to get in trouble with the law. He was stealing my mom's car, and he got into graffiti. He went to juvie. So by the time I went to college—I went straight to college out of high school and came to Berkeley—I knew that I wanted to do something in the field of juvenile justice, because I definitely could see the injustice of how he just . . . we could see his trajectory in some ways a long time coming, in terms of getting into trouble, but there was really no support for my mom. The school answers were, "We don't know what to do with him," and they just pushed him out of school at a very early age. I got to college; I wanted to be a lawyer. I wanted to work in juvenile justice. And I also remember I wrote my college admission essay, or application essay, on homelessness, and how if you're not part of the solution, you're part of the problem. I feel like I somehow in my youth developed a passion—or maybe I was born with it—for social justice work.

Left to right: Frankie Free Ramos and Carmen Valentín at FCI Dublin, California. Circa 1995. Many Bay Area supporters visited and developed close friendships with the Puerto Rican Independentistas incarcerated at FCI Dublin. Frankie Free Ramos often visited Carmen Valentín and Dylcia Pagán.

When I got to Berkeley, some other youth activists—in particular, Kahlil Jacobs Fantauzzi—started a Puerto Rican students club. It was cultural, but because of [Kahlil's] background, it was also immediately and inherently political. And I got really involved in that. In the second year of that Puerto Rican club, some of the Puerto Rican US congresspeople came out to visit the women that were incarcerated at FCI Dublin—the Puerto Rican political prisoners in particular. And they got wind of our Puerto Rican student club at Berkeley and connected us. From there, we became a very political student group and got into all kinds of [causes], not just the campaign to free Puerto Rican political prisoners, but all political prisoners, and decolonization of Puerto Rico and ending US imperialism everywhere. And so my activism and my critical consciousness just got turned on high and hasn't stopped.

Actually, we didn't meet with the congresspeople. We met with some of the organizers, and they brought a couple young people with them, and we had a meeting and they said, "Look, there are these women and they need more visitors, and you all are right here, and you can adopt each other, and you just have to start writing to them." And in some of the organizing before we started visiting them, I think we met some of the other North American anti-imperialists who were also visiting and supporting the women.

I wrote to Carmen Valentín, and so did one of my best friends, but then my other best friend Jason wrote to Dylcia and some others wrote to the other Puerto Rican women. And then we would carpool, because we were all Berkeley students. So we would time our visits together.

It was amazing. I mean, the women themselves say that our visits at that time in their imprisonment, and even after they came out of prison, were just really beautiful times, because we would have a good time. There were times when the guards would try to crack down on us and be more strict about, "You can't sit together," or "You are being too happy, you are being too loud." And I remember when they kind of changed. The women used to not have to come out to visit in uniforms, and then they had to suddenly start visiting in uniforms. I remember seeing some crackdown and some repression and some trying to dampen our joy, but we really had a lot of fun.

And yeah, we were young college students, with the drama that comes with. I remember visiting Carmen and having the drama of—I had a boyfriend, but then I met this other guy that I was really crazy about, and then at some point in there, I got pregnant. And sharing all that with them. I think they were also living vicariously through us. So it was just a lot of fun, and obviously so much learning for us to be with these OGs, who had gone through what we were going through in terms of getting politicized and being community organizers. Some of them had been teachers or, in Dylcia's case, filmmakers, all the way to becoming part of the clandestine movement. So there was so much learning in it, too.

Something that really stood out to me, because a lot of times when you get politicized, especially as folks of color and doing decolonial work, when you start learning about the role of white supremacy in it . . . I think we were really lucky to be in close contact with Marilyn Buck and Linda Evans and these North American white women who were diehard anti-imperialists and down with Black liberation and Puerto Rican liberation. Visiting the women was most impactful to my life. Their political commitment is the deepest form of solidarity that you can imagine, and it really has shaped my politics. I think there is a thin line between doing work focused solely on racial justice and having a more global and intersectional framework. Inside that frame, you understand the role of white supremacy as much greater than you think it is. That was made really concrete for me. Just knowing Linda Evans, getting to sit with her, and learning from her, and seeing the way that the women got down with each other, was amazing.

The day they came out was the best day of my life. It was surreal.

Brooke: Can you tell us about it?

Frankie: Well, we started to get wind that Clinton might actually pardon them, and I could have almost fainted. That must have been—I don't remember how far ahead of time, maybe at least a couple weeks, and it just . . . was unbelievable to me. I could not let myself believe it. I was like, "No way, No way!" Then it started to be real, because we would get updates about what were some of the sticking points. We learned that he wasn't going to pardon all of them. And the women and the men had to get together, and they were allowing them through their lawyers to have meetings and figure out whether or not those that were being offered this pardon were going to take it. One, with the condition that not all of them are going to be offered it. And two, they were going to have to renounce violence.

Both of those things were—it was not an easy decision. And so I remember also being in this limbo that was really agonizing. They were being offered clemency, but it wasn't perfect, and there were real political implications. And I could see also their integrity in terms of, they had served nineteen years and it could have been a very easy decision, but leaving some of their comrades behind and having to renounce violence was not easy for them. It went against things that they believed in. So it was a few weeks of—we didn't know for sure, and just kind of living with my heart in my throat. But at the same time, Carmen Valentín, who I would visit, was a very particular woman.

She and Dylcia, who were the two that I was the closest to—while all of this serious stuff was happening, they were like, "Okay, but if we come out, and when we come out, we got to look fly. So can I give you my ideal outfit? And can you all shop for my outfits?" So we shopped for their outfits, and it was just crazy. It was crazy. And then, I'm sure I wasn't the only one that felt this way, I could not believe it until they were actually walking out the gates. Even when they were walking out of the building and they kind of had a long walk between the building and the fence, it still felt like at any moment they could be snatched from us, right? Or that we could wake up, and it was a dream, or anything.

Then the other thing was that when they came out, they had a condition that they had to choose where they were going to go. And if they put down Puerto Rico or Chicago or New York, they had to go straight there. And so it was a little bit sad, because we would've liked to celebrate with them. Also, they could not be with each other at all. They had some parole conditions. That was the other thing: would they want to come out with parole conditions? They didn't want to have to deal with parole conditions. And that was one of the things they had to accept.

And part of the parole conditions was they could not be with each other. For Dylcia and Carmen, who were two peas in a pod all these years that they had been incarcerated—they're like yin and yang, total opposite, but just were inseparable. It was hard for us. It must have been much, much, much harder for them to imagine that they couldn't be together. So we planned a party. Somebody in our movement had a two-story flat, and because it was two different addresses, we were able to have Dylcia on one floor and Carmen on another floor. We had a party for them.

Brooke: We're almost through, but before we finish up, can you tell us a little bit about how you met the women in Out of Control, and what your relationship was to them?

Frankie: I don't know if we met at the prison or outside of prison, but when we would go visit, all of the other political prisoners would have visitors as well, so we would not only meet Linda and Laura and Marilyn, but we would meet the women visiting them. They were all organizers who were working on their campaigns and other issues. We developed our own relationships and our own friendships, and of course we were on the outside doing the organizing together. I remember the leader of the Puerto Rican student group, Kahlil—he was so well trained that he understood, even at his young tender age, the importance of developing leadership in others and developing leadership in women, young women. So he kept pushing me to be in the forefront, even though I didn't want to be. And then a lot of the older generation folks also were really invested in developing leadership in all of us young people. I remember getting invited a lot to speak at different events. I remember speaking, at least once, at Sparks Fly, where actually I was an MC, I think, with Chrystos. So, I would get invited a lot to the meetings, but especially at events, and to get on the mic at rallies. And yeah, we organized together, but I considered them mentors and friends as well.

Photo Credit: Unknown
Courtesy Frankie Free Ramos

Left to right, back: Frankie Free Ramos, Dylcia Pagán, Ray Pabon. Front: their children. Puerto Rico, 2016. Whenever Frankie and her family travel home to Puerto Rico they visit their close former-political-prisoner family.

Brooke: Can you share your thoughts about the relationship across or between the women's and queer movements and anti-imperialism, anticolonialism? What was it was like to be involved in different sectors and different pockets of the movements that you were in?

Frankie: I was always really inspired. I feel like everybody that I knew that I looked up to and who I considered close mentors, like Mirk—everybody was involved in multiple things. And it seemed like they were strategic about it, because Mirk did work on Puerto Rico, but she also did work on the Philippines, and she did work on sex trafficking. And then her close *comrade* Leslie did work that overlapped, but also really focused on Haiti. And I feel like they just were super intentional about their work and would at least be doing a couple different things at the same time. And everybody was always in the know about all of it.

So, I felt like to talk about decolonizing Puerto Rico was absolutely the same struggle as to talk about ending militarization in Okinawa, or ending sex trafficking, or ending or disrupting or dismantling heteropatriarchy. It was all just different tentacles of the same movement, but we were ultimately fighting the same beast, and I felt that what I saw was everybody really lived that. And yet, it was really because there was also a commitment to centering the leadership of those most impacted.

They didn't do it in a way where it was like one group is being all these things to all people, but they would do it in groups that were more grassroots and probably smaller. Some of them were coalitions, but always had the people most directly impacted at the table. So they weren't movements being led by these white women, lesbian women, but they were intentional about being in those spaces and just connecting all the work. And for me, that just became the norm of how I understood the work needed to happen.

PUERTO RICO: OPPRESSION AND RESISTANCE
Lucy Rodríguez Vélez and Alicia Rodríguez Vélez

Thanks to the organizers of Out of Control who, in the spirit of solidarity, reached out to two former Puerto Rican political prisoners, asking that we share a brief history of Puerto Rican resistance to US colonialism.

US military invasion of Puerto Rico

The US military invasion of Puerto Rico in 1898 altered the political, economic, social, and cultural life of all Puerto Ricans. Puerto Rico remains a colonial possession of the United States, devoid of self-determination. Following the invasion, large Puerto Rican agricultural lands were expropriated by US companies, Puerto Rican currency was devalued, and many livelihoods were destroyed.

Operation Bootstrap

Decades later, in 1948, Operation Bootstrap took center stage and promoted generous incentives to US companies to establish manufacturing plants on the island. These companies received extremely profitable tax exemptions, direct grants, and subsidies, while Puerto Rican workers were paid low wages and forced to labor in workplaces devoid of environmental or safety regulations. Operation Bootstrap yielded high profit margins for US firms, and inequality and social and economic instability for the people of Puerto Rico. Puerto Ricans found themselves producing what they do not consume and consuming what must be imported.

Forced emigration

The political, economic, social, and cultural transformation of the lives of Puerto Ricans produced a tenuous situation in the population and extreme levels of unemployment, leading to instability in colonial rule. As a result, the colonial government was forced to create a safety valve to protect its interests and thus promoted the exodus of 450,000 Puerto Ricans from our nation, whose total population in 1950 was 2,210,000. The emigration of Puerto Ricans was fostered by false promises of a better life in the US.

Left to right: Alicia Rodríguez Vélez, Juan Antonio Corretjer, Lucy Rodríguez Vélez at the Illinois State Prison at Dwight, 1983. Alicia and Lucy, sisters, were visited by renowned Puerto Rican poet and Independentista Juan Antonio Corretjer, who wrote "Boricua in la Luna," a poem about the sisters that was later popularized into a song by Roy Brown.

Measures were implemented that targeted young women of childbearing age, who were submitted to widespread controversial and highly dangerous sterilization procedures that included the use of experimental birth control pills. Without their consent or knowledge, women became guinea pigs for testing the world's first birth control pill with triple the hormone levels used in today's version of the pill. By 1970, approximately one-third of women were sterilized!

Puerto Ricans living in Chicago
In 1952, there were only 255 Puerto Ricans in Chicago. Many worked in factories and managed dangerous machinery that could

mutilate and sever limbs with presses or blades. Many worked in steel mills spewing out clouds of pollutants into the environment and into the lungs of workers. Women worked on assembly lines and in sweatshops for poor wages and in poor working conditions. Our parents were forced to work in factories and sweatshops. They worked hard for low wages, and while they could not economically provide everything our family needed, they compensated by instilling strong values in their children. They dedicated their lives to working hard, loving us unconditionally, and providing a safe environment at home.

The political, economic, social, and cultural conditions of Puerto Ricans led to the growth of militancy. Chicago's Puerto Rican community, like so many others in the United States, rebelled and resisted the violence and brutality of colonialism, racism, and exploitation. During the 1960s and 1970s, people in Chicago took to the streets demanding an end to police brutality, higher wages, affordable housing, better education, independence for Puerto Rico, freedom for Puerto Rico's political prisoners, and an end to the Vietnam War. Slogans such as "Black Power," "long live the Cuban revolution," and "free Puerto Rico" were chanted freely. A powerful wave of national and international solidarity was created.

It became evident that it was necessary to help the community take control of its institutions and, in the process, instill a sense of direction and hope. We understood that emigration transplanted colonial reality from an external colony to an internal one. We struggled to affirm our humanity while living under marginalized and objectified conditions within US society.

During this period, the Puerto Rican independence movement was targeted by the counterinsurgency program COINTELPRO, a project of the United States Federal Bureau of Investigation (FBI) that surveilled, infiltrated, discredited, and disrupted dissident political organizations. COINTELPRO was an illegal secret program. It abused power and operated without the knowledge of the media, the public, and governmental agencies intended to counter such violations.

Also during this historical period, the Puerto Rican independence movement was targeted by the Puerto Rican police's "carpetas" program that surveilled individuals and gathered and filed information on approximately 75,000 persons.

Lucy Rodríguez Vélez at the beach in Puerto Rico, 2009.

Armed struggle in the internal and external colony

The petitions to the United Nations to decolonize Puerto Rico and reliance upon the electoral system to gain independence have not been successful because both entities respond to US colonial forces.

During the 1950s, the Puerto Rican Nationalist Party, under the leadership of Don Pedro Albizu Campos, directed attacks against the president and congress of the United States, taking the struggle for independence to the seat of US power.

The resistance of the Nationalist Party, its political prisoners, and other revolutionary movements in the United States and around the world inspired our own political struggle. Our inspirations and aspirations gave revolutionary impetus to developing an armed movement of resistance.

The Fuerzas Armadas de Liberación (FALN) emerged out of this long history of Puerto Rican resistance to US colonialism. Between 1974 and 1980, the FALN would claim responsibility for attacks against military, industrial, and government installations, mainly in Chicago and New York, in order to call attention to and build support for the colonial case of Puerto Rico.

Prisoner of War status

In the early 1980s, eleven women and men, including us sisters, were captured in the United States, accused of being members of the FALN and the clandestine movement, and convicted and sentenced to the equivalent of life in US prisons for actions to end US colonial control over Puerto Rico.

After our arrest, we declared ourselves prisoners of war, asserting that the US had no jurisdiction to try us as criminals. We did not present a defense in the courtrooms. Instead, we turned our backs on the judges and demanded to be transferred to an international tribunal where we could put put the colonial case of Puerto Rico on trial.

Of course, our demands were not met, and instead we were charged with seditious conspiracy, a highly political charge that states that whenever two or more people gather to conspire to overthrow the legitimate authority of the US government by force and violence, they have committed sedition.

Movimiento de Liberación Nacional (MLN)

The Movimiento de Liberación Nacional (MLN) was created in 1977 as a coalition of Puerto Rican independence supporters and Mexican activists involved in the struggle for land rights and the socialist reunification of Mexico. During the eleven years of its existence, the MLN published theoretical and practical journals. It provided leadership to the national committee formed to defend grand-jury resisters (many of whom were MLN members). It developed campaigns for the freedom of Puerto Rico's Nationalist political prisoners who had been in prison since the early 1950s, and later the captured FALN combatants.

Among the substantial contributions of the MLN were organizing communities, building a movement of solidarity, and developing alternative institutions that served as models of decolonization and provided services to people who suffered the consequences of high levels of unemployment, mental illness, school "dropouts", and alarming consumption of drugs and alcohol.

The MLN organized and fought for liberation!

Lucy Rodríguez Vélez
Alicia Rodríguez Vélez
March 8, 2021

Alicia Rodrígez Vélez in Puerto Rico. 2003.

MY EXTENDED FAMILIA
Zulma Oliveras Vega

Out of Control (OOC) changed my life into a path of activism that comes from love, generosity, and bravery. OOC was created to bring awareness about women political prisoners, led by courageous queer women from the Bay Area. While organizing antiprison activism, focused in our lesbian communities, and organizing direct actions for the liberation of marginalized countries with anti-imperialist movements around the world, they taught me about anarchism, socialism, and that the civil rights movement is not dead.

I grew up in the town of San Germán, on the southwest part of the island of Puerto Rico. When I finished high school in 1988, I felt lost; I didn't know what to do with my life. I came from a loving working-class family; my parents are Independentistas and taught me how to use my privileges to help others in need who are marginalized. In the public school system that I attended, I was taught that after Martin Luther King Jr.'s death, the civil rights movement also disappeared, that activism for human rights was lifeless, and that Puerto Rico's fate was to accept "Uncle Sam" as our savior for "liberating" us from Spain. In our school in the '80s, I don't remember receiving historical information about Spain and the USA invading Puerto Rico. Our schools didn't give us a chance to develop our critical thinking and question authority.

Today we still don't have African or Indigenous studies departments, and the census created false ethnographic data by eliminating the categories for us Boricuas to identify as Black or Indigenous people. I didn't even learn that we could've organized in our high schools (in la FEPI) with groups similar to la FUPI (University Student Front for Independence). Meanwhile, the system injected my generation with '80s pop culture, keeping us naïve about what was really going on in our Latin American countries, victims of many coups sponsored by the US.

Feeling lost, I joined the navy during my college years in Pennsylvania—to then find out about the horrors in Vieques, our baby sister island, where the navy was experimenting with napalm and uranium bombs. I went AWOL and crossed the fence with the promise to defend the human rights of my people of Borikén.

But it wasn't until I moved from Pittsburgh to the Bay Area in 1999 that I met OOC, the organizers of Sparks Fly. I met OOC dykes through the San Francisco Dyke March (SFDM), where I spoke publicly about women political prisoners, about Vieques, and about Puerto Rico. It was through the activism of OOC and Sparks Fly that I learned we have Native American political prisoners like Leonard Peltier and Black political prisoners like Mumia Abu-Jamal. I became aware of the history of the Young Lords, the Black Panthers, Mumia, the MOVE 9, and Ramona Africa, and this really got me motivated to organize and to protest, to express myself and to educate others about the hidden history of Borikén, Puerto Rico. Connecting with indigenous communities from Chiapas and other parts of Central America, I was able to embrace my Afro-Indigenous soul without guilt or shame, and understand and embrace the brownness from my ancestry and advocate for land reparations.

I remember the weekend when Denise Alvarado introduced me to bo brown, a member of OOC. Bo took me to meet Mo Kalman, who was celebrating her birthday up north in Marin, and the rest of the OOC members were there. It was amazing to meet so many powerful women who knew about what was going on in Puerto Rico, about Palestine, about Black movements, about political prisoners and so many other important issues. It was the first time I was surrounded by an influential group like OOC, a collective of women, mostly lesbians, who were down to help the liberation struggles of other countries and marginalized communities.

Left to right: Zulma Oliveras Vega, Marilyn Buck, and Penny Schoner at FCI Dublin, California. Circa 2006.

I was able to visit Puerto Rican POW Adolfo Matos at the Lompoc federal prison, and I began to write letters to all the Boricua political prisoners. The political prisoners became my teachers, my familia. Back on the island no one talked about having POWs in the USA. I felt it was my duty to speak around the world about PR and our prisoners of war. I was willing to put my life at risk to create visibility of the colonial status that we still face. Today I still maintain a loving relationship with the ex-POWs back in PR in order to create networks of support with activists on the island.

I was also blessed to find part of my extended family in Sparks Fly, OCC, and SFDM. Because of their interest in justice, I was able to fundraise resources to travel to Palestine in 2004 with the International Solidarity Movement. My experiences with civil disobedience brought my purpose in life back to me, back to where it needs to be: to fight for our universal human rights and for our freedom, by any means necessary. Once I was able to accept that the civil rights movement is still alive and on fire, I continued collaborating with the dykes involved with Sparks Fly and SFDM. I was feeling great and full, knowing that the money raised by Sparks Fly supported the Women Women Political Prisoner Commissary Fund. The fund gave women political prisoners and Puerto Rican POWs generous donations to help them survive and alleviate certain needs while in prison. I felt that OOC and Sparks Fly women really cared about justice inside the prison complex, and the sense of justice was very clear to them. People that I love dearly introduced me to Sparks Fly and kept me under their wing: folks like bo brown, Denise Alvarado, Mo Kalman (RIP), and my dear Jane Segal. A great story I remember was that at one of the Sparks Fly fundraising events at the SF Women's Building, as the co-MC, I dressed up as Che Guevara and Jane dressed as Frida Kahlo.

These intersections of radical groups allowed me and younger generations to follow their example to create visibility and fight for our rights, including for queer trans youth back in Puerto Rico.

Altered billboard on Highway 580 in the SF Bay Area. A Women Against Imperialism action. Circa 1999.

INTERVIEW WITH DYLCIA PAGÁN

Brooke Lober

Brooke: Can you talk about your early years in the Puerto Rican independence movement, how you got involved, and anything more you want to share about that?

Dylcia: I'm a privileged Puerto Rican young woman. I'm still young [laughs]. I was raised in El Barrio, East Harlem. I was raised with a conscience because my father was a Puerto Rican nationalist. He left Puerto Rico when he was seventeen, and he never returned. I had two incredible parents. They're no longer here, but they're here in my home and in spirit.

I was given opportunities that most people in my community didn't have, so I considered that a big privilege, but by the same token, I was taught that being Puerto Rican was very important. It was the essential part of my life.

So, the movement. My father passed away when I was fifteen, but I kept active in the community. The whole issue of Culebra [the 1971 protests to remove the US Navy from Culebra] came to be in Puerto Rico. Because of my father's ties with the Nationalist Party, with my mother, we went to all the demonstrations. I learned about what was happening with the navy in Culebra, then in Vieques, and then the Puerto Rican independence movement started an organization in New York, the MPI [the Movimiento Pro-Independencia, later the Puerto Rican Socialist Party]. But they said I couldn't be a member because I wasn't born in Puerto Rico, so I said, "Okay, no problem," but I also went to all the demonstrations and got to meet everybody there. We've all become dear friends, in time.

I learned that: what does it mean to have a community? A community is a community of self-determination. Unfortunately, it still doesn't exist. No matter how much we know, those of us that have the knowledge and the enlightenment of real change, it seems to me that the system has been so powerful, especially in Puerto Rico. We are the oldest colony in the western hemisphere, right now we're in this major crisis in Puerto Rico, and it's heartbreaking.

Left to right: Ernesto Gomez Gomez and Dylcia Pagán at FCI Dublin, California. Circa 1995.

I will never change my position. Absolutely not. I think when you understand socialization, and you understand the elements of socialization, and what that endures, and what that society has created around us, we're then capable of looking at life and change in a different light. I think people like ourselves see it in a different light in order to create, to do sacrifices to have change, and I think that's what people have to learn. Change doesn't happen by marching. I tell everybody now, Black Lives Matter, Brown Lives Matter, gay people matter. Diversity. But we have to have some actions.

I'm not talking about breaking windows, or bombs. We need to do acts of resistance that open up people's minds, because otherwise, people do not respond.

Brooke: What can you share about the FALN?

Dylcia: What can I share? I always tell people that when Puerto Rico's free, I can share all the aspects of it. I can say very openly, and I say since I came out [of prison], I'm honored to say that I was a member of the FALN. Why? Because the FALN stands for Fuerzas Armadas para Liberación Nacional. Armed Forces for National Liberation.

When you commit yourself at that level [you make sacrifices]. We were an urban guerrilla movement. We had to create cells that we worked in. Some of us didn't know each other. Some of us did. We created political, military acts and opened people's minds because that was the historical moment. It's not that people who were involved in the Macheteros [the Ejército Popular Boricua, or "Boricua People's Army"], or the North Americans who were in the leftist movement, whom we were involved with, that we loved violence. No. Our world is surrounded by violence. We are oppressed by violent acts, direct or indirect. I think that was the historical moment to get involved in a struggle for national liberation.

And I knew that my commitment required some sacrifice. The sacrifice was either I die, or I was incarcerated. My biggest sacrifice was that my son was born, and I was arrested when he was two and a half years old. He's an incredible young man. He lives here, in Puerto Rico.

Our Puerto Rican national hero, who was our national poet—Juan Antonio Corretjer—he created the first socialist organization in Puerto Rico supporting armed struggle. In Puerto Rico, in the mid-'60s, we had five armed revolutionary groups in Puerto Rico. Then I think people who knew our struggle more, they emerged and broke up, and then the Macheteros came about. And that's who the FBI killed. The FBI assassinated its leader, Filiberto Ojeda Ríos, on a national Puerto Rican holiday of resistance, El Grito de Lares.

Being part of the FALN was the biggest sacrifice I made. I gave up my career, my son. But you know what? If I had to do it again, [I would]. That's part of struggle. I did almost twenty years in prison, state and federal. We couldn't see each other. We couldn't be together, the men and the women, but here, we see each other at different occasions. Then we also had six and a half years of parole, which really interfered in our life, my life, personal and professional, but I survived. I'm here. Now I'm making masks, and I'm doing other art projects and working on a documentary about the oral traditions of the municipality I live in, Loíza. Let's see what happens.

The FALN is a very important part of my life, absolutely. I'm honored. I'm honored to say that the FALN is responsible for 42 million dollars' worth of damages, which is nothing compared to what the United States government has done to our people and what they're doing today.

Right now, we have a company [Luma Energy, a private corporation taking over the power utility] that was brought in by the new governor who really wants Puerto Rico to be a state. The United States will never make us a state. I don't care how many sellouts there are, they will never make us a state. We'd have more representation than any state in the country. Of course they don't us want to be a state.

Brooke: Can you talk a little bit about your case, and your trial?

Dylcia: On April 4, 1980, at 2:20 p.m., we were arrested in Illinois. There were eleven of us in the van. No, there were ten of us—there were nine. Earlier two of our comrades had been arrested. We were going to an operation. Unfortunately, we were in an upper-middle-class area that had people there watching. This van, these crazy Puerto Ricans—they didn't see us, but they knew. They said, "These are strange people in our community." They followed us, and then they busted us.

They didn't know who we were. It was almost like one of those black-and-white movies, you know? The cops came. They put all the shotguns in the van. I said to everybody, "We're fucked." We came out, and I said, "Listen, now, we're going jogging. Don't you understand?" They said, "Get the fuck on the floor."

Then, we realized, well, here it is. We knew at that moment that we had been captured. It was an incredible experience, just the capture. I was kept at the end because I was William Morales's compañera. William was the first member of the FALN to be arrested. He escaped. He got out of the hospital, he went to Mexico, and then we got him. He's been in Cuba. My son goes to see him. We don't talk, but that's okay. My son gets to see him; that's important.

I was, of course, la compañera—you're the wife, the quote-unquote "wife," of William Morales—so I had my own private escort to the precinct. It was hilarious. I told them, "Listen, guys. What is wrong with yous?" They put cuffs on me. They put leg irons on me. I said, "I don't know how to fly." They looked at me like, *really?* When we arrived at the precinct . . . they didn't know what to do with us. They attached us to chairs, separated us from each other, and then . . . I looked. I could see the hallway. What I noticed was that [the agents were arguing] like, "They belong to us!" "No, they belong to us." It was the state and the feds, but they didn't know who the hell we were. We refused to give our names because William set up the precedents.

Most of our Puerto Rican nationalists who were arrested, who have been arrested, have been charged with seditious conspiracy. We took our position that we were prisoners of war, utilizing international law from the Geneva Conference . . . If you are captured by your enemy in a declared or undeclared war, you are allowed to declare yourselves prisoners of war. That is exactly what we did.

I believe that it overwhelmed the judges, because they'd never figured that eleven Puerto Ricans would come in and take that kind of position, both at the state and the federal level. At the same token, it was a method of also educating the judges, and the people that were there, because they didn't know what to do. I had one cop that used to go by me, and he had a sawed-off shotgun. He goes, "You know what? We can't afford these kinds of weapons," and I ignore him. He says, "Do you want to talk to me?" I say, "I have not a goddamn thing to tell you."

They tried to fingerprint us. I said, "I'm not interested in being fingerprinted." They took us to rooms. They tried to throw me down the stairs en route to our initial legal appearance at the precinct where we were being held. They tried everything, and they weren't capable of destroying none of us, our principles, our energy. They didn't allow anyone's lawyers to visit them for five days, in the precinct. . . .

For us, this was our way of setting up a trial, which was: we never recognized the jurisdiction of the United States courts by being prisoners of war. We told them very clearly that we all knew that we were in the United States of America. Puerto Rico has been at war with Spain and the US since the United States invaded us in 1898.

They were totally overwhelmed. I remember the judge, when he started—it was like holy week. He opened up the trial by saying, "When all Christians and Jews were praying, honoring the resurrection of Jesus Christ, and honoring Hanukkah, these eleven terrorists were out killing people." I said, "Wow." He even put us into the whole chronicles of the historical development of religion in the United States of America. Still, long story short, we were sentenced. First by the state, we had a state trial. Then we went to federal trial. Then we went to state custody and did three and a half years in state prison. Then we were transferred to federal custody until our release. Even in state prison, the sisters couldn't be together. They were sisters from the street. It broke our hearts. It really did. We were all separated.

Brooke: Who supported you while you were incarcerated?

Dylcia: I was supported by the National Committee to Free the Puerto Rican Prisoners of War, and my wonderful [North American women] comrades, absolutely, yes. I gave birth—it wasn't the Puerto Ricans who supported me when I gave birth. I was in Susan Tipograph's apartment! I've always had a very close relationship with my [North American women] comrades, because they visited some of our comrades, and some of our sisters visited me. So it was an ongoing exchange of commitment, struggle, and support. Mirk would visit. Edie Scripps was there. She's still in my life; she became my sister. Tipograph was William's attorney. Laura was there. Jane would visit. Who else? Sonja DeVries . . . I mean, Mirk is like my sister . . . Jane is my sister.

It's just that we created a community. Even though they supported the North Americans, they were there for us, also. I think that's the difference when you have commitment to struggle. . . . We all worked together. That's the difference. We created alliances with each other out of respect, and we did collective work. I think that's what people need to understand, that collectivity is where it's at.

People don't understand the necessity to be able to work collectively. Individualism has taken over. Materialism has taken over. I live nicely, yeah, but I'm an artist, so I can take a piece of cardboard and turn it into something. I don't have the money I used to have, but you know what? I'm in freedom.

Left to right, back row: Dylcia Pagán, Ernesto Gomez Gomez, Tania Gomez Gomez Delgado. Front row: Children. All enjoying a family visit in Puerto Rico.

SECTION 3: FCI DUBLIN: THE BEST KEPT SECRET

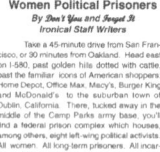

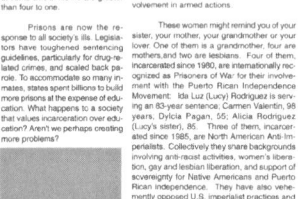

Members of Out of Control, Blue Murov and Marilyn "Mo" Kalman, writing under the pseudonyms *"Don't you"* and *"Forget It,"* created *The San Francisco Ironical*. Out of Control, LAGAI, and friends distributed the poster inside *San Francisco Chronicle* newspaper boxes. This action exposed the public to the existence of women political prisoners and POWs in FCI Dublin, California. The poster also raised the case of Mumia Abu-Jamal and the US death penalty.

REMEMBERING OUT OF CONTROL
Linda Evans

I first met my sisters from Out of Control when I was called down to the visiting room at the Washington, DC, jail. By that time I had already been locked up for three years, a whirlwind of trials and transfers. I had been on trial four times in three different states for political protest actions related to US foreign policy, racial injustice, and human rights. I was already sentenced to forty years in prison. Now I had another trial to face: I was indicted with five others in what we called the Resistance Conspiracy case.

Out of Control (OOC) supported all of us (men and women alike) in the Resistance Conspiracy case. Marilyn Kalman, an attorney and longtime member of OOC, had already suspended her life in San Francisco and moved to DC to help with our case. Now other Out of Control members traveled to DC to visit.

We were in the DC Jail for over two years. The jail was so cold during the winter that ice formed on the inside of the walls. The food was often so disgusting that we managed to eat only because there was no alternative. Rats and cockroaches skittered through our cells at night. Our jailers kept me and my codefendants separated, in solitary confinement on different tiers—although our "solitary confinement" was often subverted by other prisoners, almost all Black, who smuggled us coffee and kindness.

Visits from the outside world were few and far between. The jail visiting room had rows of two-sided cubicles separated by thick plexiglass. Embedded in the plexiglass at each visiting station was a circular metal grate to talk through. Each side of the plexiglass had a chair and a heavy old-fashioned telephone handset. Even with all these security measures, we were strip-searched before and after each visit.

Out of Control members Jane Segal and Jay Mullins journeyed from California to DC to meet us for the first time. When they entered the visiting room, I burst into a huge smile, so glad to meet them in person after sharing letters and phone calls. We couldn't hug or touch, and the time was way too short—but that was the beginning of deep friendships that still last to this day.

Out of Control made a difference in my life in several important ways. During our trial, Marilyn Kalman was a beloved and valuable ally, and her sense of humor gave us a lot of relief and laughter. Legal meetings were the only time we codefendants could see each other, and Marilyn made it possible for us to stay out of our cells for meetings long past lockdown. One of our late-night meetings involved drawing pictures of Chinese food that we could only dream of ordering! She also helped us build support in the local left community of Washington, DC.

After our trial was over, I was transferred to FCI Dublin, which was located just east of the San Francisco Bay Area, the home of Out of Control. Because there were only two federal women's prisons, it was impossible for the government to separate all of the women political prisoners. So several of us women political prisoners were at Dublin together. Women from the Resistance Conspiracy case were there along with women who fought for Puerto Rican independence and antinuclear activists. Out of Control supported and cared for all of us.

At FCI Dublin, Out of Control women continued to visit us. Here our visits were more frequent and longer. We could visit outside in a small, fenced yard. We could eat vending-machine food! And hugs were allowed—as long as they were brief, and only at the beginning or end of a visit. These visits were a delight in the wasteland of our drab prison existence. Out of Control's support was direct and enthusiastic; it was both personal and political. The women braved bumper-to-bumper Bay Area rush-hour traffic to visit. They raised money to send to our commissary accounts so we could buy extra food, as well as arts-and-crafts supplies. We celebrated birthdays and holidays together in that visiting room, and they brought others to visit, including my cellmate's children.

Linda Evans, incarcerated for sixteen and a half years, eleven of those at FCI Dublin, California. Many Bay Area activists, including several Out of Control members, visited Linda and became lifelong friends. Photo Credit: Prison photo Courtesy Out of Control Collection

Perhaps most important to us, Out of Control connected us to the larger activist community and helped us relate to emerging political movements. They read our solidarity statements aloud at demonstrations, published our writings, and made our voices a part of the struggles of that time. For us, as political prisoners, this connection was our lifeblood, and Out of Control was a beloved and invaluable connector.

For a few years, spearheaded by several of us political prisoners, women at FCI Dublin organized an AIDS peer education and counseling group. We sponsored a weeklong walkathon on the prison track, raising money from friends and family to support AIDS services. Our Prisoners Fight AIDS Walkathon donated to a San Francisco hotel that housed HIV+ people, and to children with AIDS at Oakland Children's Hospital. Out of Control publicized the walkathon, solicited donations, and donated money themselves. About half the women prisoners at Dublin participated in the walkathon. Many others made donations from their meager prison salaries. We were able to raise several thousand dollars for AIDS services. The generosity and caring shown by the incarcerated women helped break down negative stereotypes about people in prison. Just as importantly, there was a palpably different feeling at FCI Dublin during the week of the walkathon: women inside felt connected to the outside world, and we felt the pride, joy, and self-worth of giving to others. It was a special time, and Out of Control played an important role in making our walkathon a success.

Out of Control was amazingly creative in educating the public about political prisoners. In one action, they wrapped hundreds of copies of the *San Francisco Chronicle* (bought from newspaper boxes) with a new front page sporting an eye-catching headline: "Best Kept Secret in the Bay Area: 8 Women Political Prisoners Held in Dublin, CA." Pictures of all the women political prisoners adorned the *San Francisco Ironical* front page. The newspapers, wrapped with the *Ironical* cover page, were then returned to the boxes. Hundreds of Bay Area residents enjoyed their newspaper that morning with a bonus front page, and news of the existence of women political prisoners reached new people.

On January 20, 2001, I was granted my release from prison by President Clinton on his last day in office. Now I began to experience the sisterhood of Out of Control in the outside world. Just a few months after my release, Marilyn Kalman arranged for me to speak at San Francisco's Dyke March. This was the first gay pride celebration I had ever attended. I had a chance to talk with thousands of women about women in prison and political prisoners. I remember being up on the stage, staring out at that huge crowd of women. I felt nervous, overwhelmed—hoping I could inspire them to support women prisoners. What I also remember about that day was the contingent of Dykes on Bikes, and a flatbed truck with music blaring and women dancing topless. After sixteen years in prison, this was quite something to behold!

Another important OOC activity was Sparks Fly—a benefit to raise awareness and support for women political prisoners. Artists, musicians, and poets donated their time and artwork to raise money for the Women Political Prisoner Commissary Fund, a joint project of LAGAI (Lesbians and Gays Against Intervention) and OOC. People came together from all over the Bay Area to honor women political prisoners, and to celebrate resistance. I so deeply appreciate the love and hard work of all the women in Out of Control—their support changed my life in prison, and I'm forever grateful.

Left to right: Eve Goldberg and Linda Evans in their home in Santa Rosa. 2006.

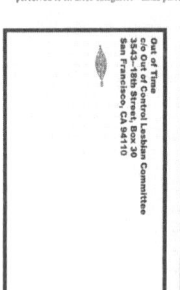

This sample *Out of Time* headlines the 2001 SF Dyke March, which was dedicated to women in prison. Linda Evans spoke to thousands of dykes in Dolores Park and urged everyone to remember those sisters inside and work for their release. The other headlines are international: the occupation of Palestine and the extreme oppression of LGBT people in Egypt.

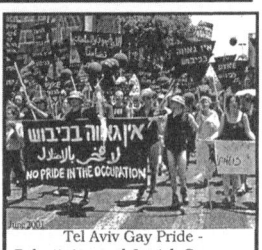

WHEN THE PRISON DOORS ARE OPENED, THE REAL DRAGON WILL FLY OUT

Linda Evans

A quilt piece made by Linda Evans. The embroidered text reads, "When the prison doors are opened, the Real Dragon will fly out." —Ho Chi Minh. Linda started quilting inside prison and became an accomplished quilt artist. She made this wall hanging while inside FCI Dublin.

CLANDESTINE KISSES

Marilyn Buck

For Linda and her love

Kisses
bloom on lips
which have already spoken
stolen clandestine kisses

a prisoner kisses
she is defiant
she breaks the rules
she traffics in contraband women's kisses
a crime wave of kisses
bittersweet sensuality
flouting women hating satraps
in their prison fiefdoms
furious
that love
cannot be arrested

First published in *Inside/Out* (City Lights Books, 2012)

FOR MARILYN BUCK (1947–2010)
Tanya Napier and Gemma Mirkinson

For those that know of Marilyn Buck beyond the propaganda of the state, she is a revolutionary hero, a freedom fighter, a political icon. For those that knew her personally, she was something deeper: a feminist, an artist, a skilled translator, a teacher, a yogi, a militant, a poet, an anti-imperialist, a staunch antiracist, a sister, a friend, a grandma, a comrade. For the two of us, she was our godmother, a mentor, a confidant, our family.

Photo Credit: Prison photo
Courtesy Penny Schoner Collection

Marilyn Buck was incarcerated for fifteen years at FCI Dublin. In addition to being an artist, a dedicated freedom fighter, and always an organizer, Marilyn was a remarkable friend to all who knew her. Many Bay Area activists, including Out of Control and LAGAI members, visited Marilyn and developed long-lasting friendships.

Until Marilyn died, we spent most of our lives traveling to FCI Dublin, where she was imprisoned as a political prisoner. We grew up with her and grew with her. Loving someone who is in prison is not easy, as so many in America will know. It is a quick study in the cruelty of the state. The experience of visiting and loving people in prison like Marilyn has left an indelible mark on how we live our lives and view the world. Nothing is as blatantly vengeful as how the government treats political prisoners, yet to know these people, to have known Marilyn, is to understand a life devoted to resistance and resilience.

Marilyn spent almost half of her sixty-two years in prison. Born in Texas, she began her antiracist activism as a teenager. As a college student at UC Berkeley, she joined Students for a Democratic Society and was active in establishing women's liberation as a core part of the SDS platform. The prevalence of international liberation struggles was deeply impactful to Marilyn's political development. She actively fought against US foreign intervention, worked in solidarity with national liberation struggles and the Black liberation movement, and contributed to political propaganda. As political movements in the US became more militant, so did Marilyn. In 1973, she was convicted of purchasing ammunition with a false ID and given ten years. Marilyn served some time and, after being granted a furlough, never returned. She remained in the political underground, and in 1985 was recaptured and charged with several crimes, including participation in the escape of Black political prisoner Assata Shakur. She was also convicted in the Resistance Conspiracy case in connection with several bombings at the US Capitol, the National War College, and the South African Embassy. She was given an eighty-year sentence.

Throughout her incarceration, Marilyn remained connected to the outside world and to politics. She never stood still. She evolved constantly. She received several degrees, produced poems, essays, and ceramics, and taught GED preparation, writing, history, and yoga.

After over twenty-five years in prison, Marilyn was finally given a parole date for August 8, 2010. As plans were being made for her release, she was diagnosed with a rare form of uterine cancer. Due to the gravity of her illness, her lawyer and dear friend Soffiyah Elijah was able to secure an earlier date, and she was released on July 15, 2010. On August 3, just three short weeks after her release from prison, Marilyn died in her home in Brooklyn surrounded by her friends and family.

As her goddaughters, we often talk about how similar and yet how very different our experiences with Marilyn were. Perhaps one of her great gifts was her ability to connect intimately and uniquely with each person she formed a relationship with.

Gemma writes:

Marilyn helped me navigate almost every stage of my life. She helped me untangle feelings of love, family dynamics, personal challenges, and political development. She was never patronizing or preachy, but instead had a distinct way of being simultaneously stern and tender. She allowed me space to talk through decisions and ideas. She forced me to look at my actions and how they impacted a scenario or ideology. She helped me understand the personal power of disobedience, how to trust my gut, to feel confident in my voice, to challenge feelings of inadequacy, and to be open to growth and change. I stumbled over so many life questions with her over that small table in the FCI Dublin visiting room. When I had the special opportunity of being with Marilyn in New York in the last weeks of her life, I remember holding her hand for hours, soaking up the smoothness of her skin, eating with her, listening to music, laughing, and, probably most importantly, living next to her in freedom.

The night before she died, Marilyn said to me: "No one is going to tell you to leave here, and no one is going to tell me to leave. We are home."

Tanya writes:

I remember what it felt like every Sunday, that was our day, driving out to visit her. I would start out nervous, insecure that I was going to see this woman who I admired so much, who in my mind was somewhat of a celebrity. I would notice how much the inmates and even some guards respected her. Waiting for her to walk through those doors felt like I was waiting to open a present on my birthday or Christmas. Once she sat at the table and we began to speak to each other, holding each other's hands, I would melt. I'd feel safe and secure, and truly loved. They say the bond that's made between mother and daughter can never be broken, and since she took care of me as a baby, we were bonded, and you could feel it. I never understood or realized how much I meant to her, and I only hope that she understood and realized how much she meant to me. The day I brought my own daughter, Ayla, to visit her for the first time, there was no fear or insecurity. I was so proud to finally make her a grandmother. Once my child was old enough, we visited regularly, and she would take Ayla by the hand and walk off with her. I would sit there watching them, and it warmed my heart. She would take Ayla to go to the kids' room, and I would wait patiently, because I knew it was important for them to have their own bond. I am so grateful that I have those moments to share and remember with Ayla, and that Ayla can remember Mama Marilyn and be proud.

This year marked ten years since Marilyn passed. Her community had hoped to have a celebration of her life, to gather and laugh and eat and read her poetry out loud. Instead, on her tenth anniversary, America was five months into the COVID-19 pandemic and deep into a summer of political rebellion addressing systemic racism, police murder, and Black liberation. We like to think that the political moment was its own version of a Marilyn Buck celebration and can't help but imagine how excited she would be to sit and talk about it all.

Left to right: Ayla Pittman, Marilyn Buck, Tanya Napier.
Tanya and Ayla visited Marilyn every week.

Left to right, back row: Ida McCray, Marilyn Buck, Kwame Ture, Linda Evans, Carmen Valentín. Front row: Ernesto Gomez Gomez, Dylcia Pagán, Laura Whitehorn at FCI Dublin. Circa 1996.

MOON BEREFT

Marilyn Buck

Beyond razor-wired walls
the moon shimmers in the late summer sky
spills over in pale brightness
to draw me into its fullness
washing my eyes in quicksilver

Now, in a heavy-lidded cell
moon-bereft nights leave me weeping
tears well up in dry cratered wounds
despair rises
dark and irradiated
to swallow starlight
and spit it out
like steel needles
that incite my loneliness

My soul careens off cell walls
wails till pain tires
and the pale moon of memory
appears to call me home

July 1990
First published in *Inside/Out* (City Lights Books, 2012)

A STORY IN CELEBRATION OF THE INTIFADA
Marilyn Buck

David, son of Israel, slew Goliath
he smiled that one so small
could defeat one so large

he took Goliath's house
walked in his shoes
and ate at his table

David, son of Israel, became Goliath
greedy, grasping, merciless
he thumbed his nose at
the ageless people
of the olive groves and desert

remembering only that he had been small
he forgot

the daughters and sons of Palestine
do not forget
that a stone is not just a stone
lying in the rubble of their homes
it becomes a missile
ululating resistance
raising a storm of liberation.

First published in *Hauling Up the Morning* (Red Sea Press, 1990)

SCENE FROM THE INTIFADA

Laura Whitehorn

Drawing made by Laura Whitehorn in the DC Jail, 1989.

INTERVIEW WITH JUDY SIFF
Brooke Lober

In different ways, each of the members of Out of Control participated in leftist movements and related social justice projects before, during, and after their time in the organization. Judy Siff was a political prisoner herself, and when she was released, she went to work with Out of Control. Today she's a clinical therapist with a private practice, and she also runs a support group for formerly incarcerated people. This interview begins with a discussion of Judy's time in the legendary Weather Underground Organization.

Brooke: What was it like, living underground?

Judy: We lived in different cities around the country. Everyone was in a collective; the collectives met and had political discussion. We would read and study, much like other movement people . . . In some ways it wasn't very different from how anybody else lived. If you looked at us, we were just like anybody else on the quiet or on the not-so-quiet streets where we lived, but we were not in the middle of demonstrations. We did a lot of studying, we did a lot of reading; I went back to school to become a nurse, which I did briefly. And that's a whole other story, but other people did that, too. I mean, we had to work, we had to support ourselves.

I was part of the internal writing and struggle within Weather, especially around women; it was very important to me. There were the internal processes, and then there were the political statements that got communicated—and they weren't always quite the same. What we said about women publicly was kind of liberal, in the sense that it was positive, but it wasn't exactly a revolutionary or fundamentally challenging perspective on women. But internally, women were encouraged and developed into leadership and so on. This did not extend to recognizing and/or explicitly developing lesbian/gay leadership and politics. There were differences in terms of how to develop analysis and strategies. There were differences about "working class versus revolutionary nationalist" perspectives. The Hard Times conference was when it all exploded, because that was when people from revolutionary movements really became publicly critical of the politics that were expressed within Prairie Fire organization, influenced by the Weather Underground. So it all came out at that time.

For me, I was part of an internal section within Weather that agreed with the criticisms of the Hard Times conference. Many people were critical about all different kinds of things that led in different directions—but I was part of the group that ultimately was instrumental in the end chapter of Weather.

I was really moved and excited by Hard Times. Because it explained to me some of the discontents that I felt about what was going on, or what wasn't going on politically, the meaning of our statements, the meaning of our actions, the decrease in the actions that we did over the years, and the focus on things that weren't necessarily those things that I wanted to focus on. And so the criticisms that I heard became ones that I thought deeply about and, along with other people, starting developing internally as well. On the surface, Hard Times wasn't literally about the Weather Underground, but from within Weather, we understood those criticisms to be about us and developed them internally as well, holding our leaders accountable for it. And that's what happened! Eventually the result was that we declared the organization over.

Brooke: So when did you, and how did you, end up on trial and in prison?

Judy: We essentially closed down the Weather Underground and became a splinter, the Revolutionary Committee. The FBI did not believe it was closed down, and they were seeking to find the well-known WUO leadership; we were infiltrated. Their agent was successful in encouraging us to develop an action against the office of State Senator Briggs. That was their setup.

That's how we got arrested. We were arrested in Houston, Texas, because it was the location of the National Women's Conference. That was 1977.

It was simultaneously a gathering of every right-wing organization that you could imagine, so that led to our decision to go there, too. The setup plan was a potential retaliatory action if something bad came down. As I said, we were infiltrated, and the agents were there with us. After we had gone to monitor one of the right-wing mass meetings, we came back out to our car, followed by a group of rapidly moving men—who drew their guns and arrested us on the spot. Then we were arrested. It was just like that. We were taken to the Houston County Jail. We were kept there for about a week. Once we got over the initial shock of arrest, that was the most frightening week of the entire incarceration, might I say.

Brooke: Why was that the most frightening?

Judy: Because two days later, a female prisoner from my cell block approached me saying, "You know, you don't look suicidal." I said, "Suicidal?" I was stunned. They said, "Yeah. They told us you were suicidal, and we should watch you." So that was scary. In any case, we eventually got sent back to California. I was in Sybil Brand County Jail with one of my codefendants. There were five of us: two women, three men—all of us were held in pretrial at county jail for over a year. And then eventually we two women went up to California Institution for Women for year two. Then I got sent up to Seattle to resolve the Seattle charge. Then I eventually wound up in Dublin/Pleasanton FCI for the rest of my prison time.

Brooke: How did your life change during that time, and how did your thinking change during that time?

Judy: Well, it slowed things down. It gave me a lot of time to read. I've never read as much in my life as I did while in prison. There were a few other people in prison for political reasons, but most were not at all. It was the first time I had an abundance of day-to-day relationships with people of color, because that's who

I was in prison with. This gave me more of an opportunity to get a sense of what people's lives were like than I ever had—meeting the families, the babies, the children, hearing personal stories and everyday experiences. It was a profound and meaningful experience to me.

I think in a lot of ways being in prison for me was different from how it was for most of the people around me. Certainly it was different from the political prisoners who by now have spent more than thirty or forty years in prison! But just as different in another way from all the social prisoners doing two, four, ten years—for crimes of survival. Don't get me wrong, my four years was a long enough time, but at the end of the day, it wasn't all that long. For me, the fact that I was there not because I was a victim of society, but because of the result of conscious adult choices that I made, just made a difference in terms of how that experience was for me. I was certainly glad to get out, oh yes. But I didn't experience it as "how could this happen to me."

Brooke: Were you lesbian-identified while you were incarcerated?

Judy: That's difficult to answer. I would say yes: yes, I absolutely considered myself a lesbian. I considered myself a lesbian since shortly after I broke up with my husband. Even then, I had had many thoughts about who I had been all along. However, when I entered Weather, I didn't live as a lesbian. I didn't have a lesbian relationship for a long time and did occasionally have relationships with men. So when I was in prison, I had conflicted thoughts about what I wanted to say to the world about who I was. Inside myself, I knew I was a lesbian, but I didn't feel like it was right to claim that status, so I didn't. Then when I got out of prison that was no longer a problem for me.

I wanted people to support me for being as complicated as I am. That's just what it is. Shortly after I got out of prison, I met and fell in love with my partner, who I've been with for the last thirty-seven years. So that made my public identity simple in that kind of way.

Brooke: What did you do when you were released?

Judy: I got out in October 1981. The first thing I wanted to do was go to New York to see my family. I arrived in New York three weeks later, on October 20, 1981. I was required to see a probation officer (PO) immediately after I got there. The PO was supposed to come and see me in my brother's home. I remember reading the *New York Times* that morning, noticing a headline about an unusual Brinks robbery involving both Black people and white people, and planned to read it later. Then the probation officer arrived at the house, and before even sitting down, he immediately put pictures of David Gilbert and Kathy Boudin in front of my face and said, "Know these people?" I was beyond stunned. That's how I found out about them.

Anyway, it was a very difficult reentry that way because that was literally the first thing that happened right after I got out. I was in New York for a while and then went back to California. Of course, I became involved in some of the support work for them, even though there were some limitations on me because I was on probation. It was supposed to be for five years.

Then I got involved in Prairie Fire. Within the organization, there were different directions that the work took. I was involved in US-based Black liberation and anti-Klan work. Other sections of the organization worked on Puerto Rico, Native American solidarity. People did Native American work and women's work, particularly with Women Against Imperialism.

Brooke: What brought you toward deciding to be a therapist, and when did that happen?

Judy: I decided I was gonna go back to school. The thing about therapy was I was in therapy myself, and it was very meaningful to me, and I realized it was something I could do. And it touched me because I think growing up, if it had been a different set of circumstances, I probably would've become a teacher. But that just isn't the way I was pushed and shaped. Therapy wouldn't have occurred to me when I was younger.

But in prison, people talked to me. People would come to me and tell me their stories, and I realized that I liked to listen. I liked to hear people's stories, and it would mean a great deal to me that people seem to take some comfort in being listened to. So I decided that's what I wanted to do, but I also realized that revolution was further away than I once hoped and that I needed to do something that was meaningful along the way as well as wanting that to happen—and I could see the difference that it made to people just to be heard. So I did it. I didn't join Out of Control till I was back here, in San Francisco—in 1997.

We don't want to ever forget the political prisoners, and they do get forgotten. You might want to notice when you go places where prisoners have been talked about—see if the political prisoners are mentioned or not. Mostly, I would say, not. I mean, it's amazing. Herman Bell got out after forty-five years. Jalil is not out. The MOVE prisoners, most of them, are not out.[1] A lot of them are still there, and it's going on fifty years—forty, fifty years; their entire lives. And I think what's good for prisoners in general is good for the political prisoners—and what's good for political prisoners is good for all prisoners.

---

[1] The MOVE prisoners and Jalil Muntaqim were released after this interview took place. See Ed Pilkington, "Chuck Sims Africa Freed: Final Jailed Move 9 Member Released From Prison," *The Guardian*, February 7, 2020, https://www.theguardian.com/us-news/2020/feb/07/chuck-sims-africa-move-9-freed-philadelphia, and Ed Pilkington, "Former Black Panther to Be Released After 49 Years in Prison," *The Guardian*, September 24, 2020, https://www.theguardian.com/us-news/2020/sep/24/jalil-muntaqim-former-black-panther-to-be-released-49-years-prison.

THIRTEEN SPRINGS

Marilyn Buck

had you planted a tree
to fill in the deep well
of my absence
that tree would be
thirteen springs high
high enough to relieve
the relentless sun of incarceration
strong enough to bear
the weight of children
who might have been born
had I not been seized
from your life and plunged
into this acid-washed crypt
of perpetual loss
and high-wired vigilance

but there is no tree
that stands in my place
to harbor birds and changing winds
perhaps someone will plant
a willow a eucalyptus
or even a redwood
any tree that will
in thirteen years more
bear fruit and provide shelter

August 1997

INTERVIEW WITH JAY MULLINS
Brooke Lober

Jay: Out of Control was a group of lesbians in San Francisco who came together to shut down the Lexington Control Unit. It was the first high-security unit built specially for women, in the basement of the federal prison in Lexington, Kentucky. For me, Out of Control was a place where I could be an out butch dyke, and do political work, and be surrounded by lesbians and other butch dykes, like bo [brown] and like Mo [Kalman].

Out of Control worked together with white progressive groups and national liberation organizations, whose organizations had prisoners of war and political prisoners doing extremely lengthy prison sentences. But it felt like homophobia was tolerated, and being a butch was seen as more or less a white issue, and "it wasn't the most important issue we're dealing with." It was comforting to have Out of Control, strong lesbian sisters that had our backs and supported us.

We're talking about the '80s, right? It was Reagan: prison populations increased 90 percent, AIDS, queers could be ticketed for kissing. Being an out butch dyke, a lesbian, was unacceptable. Progressive movements were not immune to sexism or homophobia, and at that time being queer and being visible was always seen as a white, liberal, San Francisco thing.

This notion was difficult for us to deal with, being lesbians committed to fighting for freedom of all political prisoners. Straight people couldn't understand that we didn't wanna be men, don't wanna be men; we're women who love women, we're lesbian, we're butches, that is who we are.

Bo had done prison time, is a former political prisoner, but still was overlooked and not given the respect she should have been given. It was hurtful. I'm just reliving those feelings: showing up in Chicago with bo, showing up in DC with Mo, just the two of us walking into the room, and people would look at us like, WHAT!—it was unusual, as visible butches, to even be there, in a space of internationalist leftist organizing. We were proud. We felt like, "This is who we are, and we're here to support the freedom of political prisoners, and we're here to do whatever we can do to that end."

Laura Whitehorn designed this bookmark. Out of Control and other activists in the Bay Area and nationally sold the bookmarks to support the political prisoners.

Over time, our working relationships got better because we struggled for change in a principled way, and we got respect from the progressive white organizations and national liberation organizations in return. Out of Control was in it for the long haul; we showed what we were made of in terms of our activism and commitment. In the long run, we developed some lasting friendships and mutual respect.

Brooke: Were there other queer people in the movements that you sometimes met up with?

Jay: Oh, sure. We worked with queers who were members of the national liberation organizations, as well as progressive groups in San Francisco. We worked with LAGAI, a radical queer group. While organizing to shut down the Lexington Control Unit, we worked with groups in New York, Chicago, and Lexington, KY, that came from various women's and lesbian communities—some were mixed Black and white groups—as well as with the Free Norma Jean Croy committee.

Brooke: You mentioned that you thought you lived through an "evolution" in queer politics. What do you think the evolution was?

Jay: I believe the evolution happened while working side by side for freedom of POWs and political prisoners and struggling for lesbian and gay visibility with people in the committees and organizations with whom we worked. Queer organizations started coming out more, like ACT UP, and also LAGAI, who worked in [solidarity movements]. Gay people were present and working in a lot of groups and organizations. I think that gay people inside the national liberation movements, like Puerto Rican, Black liberation, and New African Movement activists who were gay, started coming out and being more visible. The pressure from these gay activists helped shift and change the perceptions and attitudes toward queers in the progressive and solidarity movements. It connected the struggles for liberation, self-determination, with homophobia.

Brooke: I know that Jewelle Gomez and Chrystos and Angela Davis and a lot of well-known artists, including a lot of lesbians of color, performed at Sparks Fly. What was the connection?

Jay: There is a long list of performers, activists, writers, musicians who contributed, yes. They were at Sparks Fly because they were committed to supporting women political prisoners and they wanted to help raise money for the commissary fund. They had radical feminist politics and understood the reality of prisons in this country.

Brooke: It sounds like one of the ways that you bridged the worlds between radical lesbian movements and queer culture was, for example, at Gay Day. At least in my experience, Pride is supposed to be fun! But you came with a really serious message. How did that feel, to bring the story of racism, repression, and political prisoners to gay and feminist celebration spaces?

Jay: Out of Control went to Gay Day—and we were out as lesbians, but also out with our brand of politics. We were like: "There are political prisoners and prisoners of war in the United States. These are their names, and these are their stories. Some of them are lesbians." I think it connected us to the queer community. Gay Day made us feel whole, like there's a place for both things to happen: talk to queers about prisons, prisoners, and politics in a gay atmosphere.

We go to Gay Day in celebration of life, in celebration of being gay, but at the same time, you've got gay people doing time for political actions. They're not just doing time; they're doing a lot of time. For example, using a false ID to buy two guns and two boxes of ammunition—someone who is not political may get ten years total. But Linda got ten years maximum on every count: maximum forty years. A proven false accusation of murder put political prisoner Geronimo Ji-Jaga Pratt in prison for over twenty-five years. We would share these stories that expose the state in its attempt to destroy our social movements through long mandatory sentencing and outright lies.

People could get behind our message. We could move them down the path of political consciousness by connecting, making links between our oppression as gay and lesbian people and the oppression of militants who were gay and straight. I think people wanted to hear our message, and it helped change their understanding. Some thought that Gay Day was a big drunk party and everyone's gonna have sex at the end. And I don't think that's what it ever was. It was always a celebration of liberation, to me. So linking repression, political prisoners, and gay liberation together was natural.

Brooke: I want to ask you about before Out of Control. How did you come to political consciousness? What was your earlier political activism?

Jay: I was raised north of LA in a farming community by Southern fundamentalist Christian parents during the Vietnam era, Black Power, and Watts. In high school I began reading radical periodicals: the *Berkeley Barb* and the *Oracle*. Reading them opened my mind and changed my world. I also "came out" in high school.

Soon after graduating I moved to Portland, Oregon. I was attending Portland State when I met my friend Julie, who introduced me to her lesbian collective household where my early activism began to broaden. Her household along with other friends opened the Mountain Moving Café, an activist and community center. It offered good food at low prices, a women's only night, a kids' corner, and had an attached bookstore. I participated in demonstrations like International Women's Day, spray-painted on walls, and joined various groups supporting a variety of causes and people. I worked on a committee that brought Puerto Rican prisoner of war Lolita Lebrón to Portland after twenty-five years in federal prison.

Brooke: So, it was in lesbian communities, doing feminist demonstrating and public activism. I remember you saying, in the interview we did before, that you had been supporting bo brown when bo was incarcerated.

In 1990, Alison Bechdel published a *Dykes to Watch Out For* comic about the Resistance Conspiracy Defendants. Out of Control created a flyer using her comic strip, and Out of Control, LAGAI, and their friends passed out five thousand at Gay Pride.

Jay: Yes. We were a lesbian group of activists; some of the women had lived in Seattle, and had known bo and the George Jackson Brigade. We started by doing material support: writing letters, petitions, and that kind of stuff, putting out leaflets with information about her and the Brigade. We would visit with bo by telephone during our meetings. And that's how I met bo, by supporting her inside. When she got out, we became close friends and did political work together in Out of Control for many years. Our group also worked with Indigenous peoples in Portland who were struggling for water rights and fishing rights of the Columbia River. These experiences helped to broaden my political views and develop and expand my understanding of the meaning of political prisoners and national liberation.

Brooke: When did you move to the Bay Area?

Jay: I moved to San Francisco in 1981 and continued to do political work with various groups. I participated in petitioning, organizing, and demonstrations calling for freedom for the Puerto Rican prisoners of war, political prisoners like Marilyn Buck, the New York Three, and other political people held in prisons around the country. I also began visiting people in prison. I had met Silvia Baraldini a few years before she was incarcerated, so when she was sent to FCI Pleasanton [Dublin] I started visiting her there. After Silvia, Susan, and Alejandrina were sent to the sensory-deprivation unit in Lexington, KY, is when bo, Jane, Mirk, and I met to decide a response, and that was the Committee to Shut Down the Lexington Control Unit.

Brooke: What do you remember the most about doing this support work?

Jay: I think meetings, our *Out of Time* newsletter, petitions, writing letters, and visiting, a lot. That was a big deal, visiting. It gave me an inside look at how the women inside lived day to day. It was, I believe, mostly monotonous and boring, and the guards were intrusive inside, and the women were isolated from family and their community. However, it wasn't always that. The political prisoners worked while inside, educating themselves and others about AIDS as well as helping some women to learn to read. They lived their politics inside. I believe it gave me a real empathetic look at what most people have to deal with psychologically, emotionally, in prison.

Visiting was very special for me. I took my son to visit Silvia and my daughter with me to visit Marilyn in FCI Dublin.

Brooke: What do you think was special about lesbians being able to do those visits and make those connections? There were different political prisoner-support groups, and Out of Control was one of the few that was lesbian identified.

Jay: It was a big deal to be able to visit Laura, and Linda, Silvia, Susan, and Marilyn, who were incarcerated in prisons around the country and are remarkable women. I visited to offer my love and support to the sisters inside, to ease the isolation, to connect with them personally, and politically to connect them with the outside. Prison is meant to break your spirit, to cut you off from human contact and interaction. I think being "out" and in the visiting room was a statement of queer solidarity and gave moral support to the lesbian political prisoners. Personally, I have a lot of gratitude for being able to go to different parts of the country and visit. Over the years, my conversations with the women political prisoners helped transform my understanding of the world and helped me grow personally and politically.

Brooke: I want to ask you before we finish: I know that when we started talking, before I was recording, you were talking a little bit about the legacy of Out of Control, and looking back from the perspective of today. Can you say a little bit about how you reflect on that time now, and how you would want others to learn about it from the vantage point of today?

Jay: The legacy of Out of Control is it being a part of a movement that freed some people from prison, made an impact on the social conscience, and [made] a difference in the lives of political prisoners and others living inside prison. We were a part of exposing and changing the queer community's understanding of political prisoners and prisons. We have witnessed these ideas grow and develop through prison activism and prisoner support.

Right now, people are organizing, demonstrating, resisting, struggling to change institutions and systems in our country. I feel my work within a small group like Out of Control has an impact, and that small groups can grow, connect with others, and we can make a difference together. The proverb "Mighty oaks grow from little acorns" is fitting.

OUT OF CONTROL, IN CONVERSATION: JAY, JANE, PENNY, AND JUDY

Brooke Lober

Brooke: What was it like for you all to work on the campaign to close Lexington?

Jay: As dykes, as lesbians, it was interesting. We felt that [as] lesbians, we faced a lot of homophobia. Not everyone thinks that it's okay, right? [laughs] A lot of men don't think it's okay to be dykes, right? So—

Jane: In 1987.

Jay: In 1987. But ultimately it was really good. We felt that we provided a lot of consciousness-raising for the men and women in the national organizations and the churches that were part of the coalition. I mean, in every facet of political work, to be queer—it took time for people to understand us, but all in all, we've made long-term friends with the people we met through this work, and mutual respect.

Jane: I think we did, yeah. We did make friends and mutual respect. The people in Chicago, in particular.

Jay: And we met a lot of people. We worked with the MLN [Movimiento para Liberación Nacional], the Free Puerto Rico Committee here—who else? United Churches of Christ.

Jane: We also connected with other lesbians who were doing work around political prisoners at the time, in New York and Chicago. One group was called Queers United in Support of Political Prisoners, QUISP.

Jay: They also did ACT UP work.

Jane: We developed relationships, friendships . . . Out of Control worked closely with people from Chicago and New York. We placed two big ads [about the women political prisoners at Lexington] in *Off Our Backs* and *Gay Community News*, which were distributed nationally.

Jane: We would collect signatures from academics and elected officials, people who were heads of nonprofits. You know, typical campaigns, where you send letters out, we get money back and get signatories, and then we'd publish a big ad that was about the transfer of women political prisoners to Lexington. That was the National Campaign.

One thing I remember about the feeling of participating in that coalition—I'm a lesbian, but I can pass for straight. I could then, and I still could if I wanted to. So, to be honest, for me it's a different experience than for people who were butch. And there were a number of butch women in our group, including Jay and bo, and Deeg and Mo Kalman. That was very educational for me: to be in situations where I'm looked at differently than Jay or bo.

But I think that it worked out well. And Mo and Jay, and bo, at different times, went to Chicago for national meetings, [and I think that] it broke down a lot of barriers, and that people really came together over that. I thought it was very good.

I mean, homophobia is still here. You know, it was certainly around us more in 1987, but we were in the Bay Area, so we were lucky. In many ways because we had a lot of support from other people who were more accepting of us.

Judy: Yeah, and I think that Chicago—I think they would say, about us, that we provided a place for people to raise their consciousness around queers.

Jane: I totally agree. I think they would say that as well.

Brooke: It sounds like you did a lot of consciousness-raising within the movement. Why was it important to specifically have a lesbian group doing political prisoner work at that time or later?

Jay: Some of the political prisoners were lesbians. Our involvement lessened the isolation they felt being queer and political inside prison. And I think that that was a really important aspect of it, for me. Could have been us, you know, in this way; our political work, we just didn't happen to take that step at the moment that some of these women did. Judy did, but I didn't, and

I feel like that—you just feel a bond with that. So, I think that's mirroring them on the outside.

Judy: Don't you think there's a connection around invisibility? I mean, women inside, especially lesbians, were not visible to the world. Women in prison are not visible to the world. Especially back then, but today. And lesbians—especially then, but also today—are not visible. And that was just part of the connection: let the world tear down the walls. Let people see. Let people know who they are and who we are.

Free Women Political Prisoners banner made by Penny Schoner, a member of Out of Control. It was displayed at Sparks Fly and other events about the women prisoners.

Jay: Right.

Brooke: How was your work perceived in the gay or queer movement? That you were doing political-prisoner work? What was that like?

Jane: Well, the Dyke March was started by some of our friends. The Dyke March gave us visibility too. At the second or third one, very early on, there were seven thousand people, and I was given a chance to say something about political prisoners—women, lesbian, political prisoners—to all those people. And I was terrified. But anyway, I do remember doing it, and I do remember the response from masses of people—a lot of people hadn't known what we were talking about. For example, people had never heard of Linda Evans. So, one time, at Gay Pride, I was carrying a sign, *FREE LINDA EVANS*, and these dykes would come up to us and say, "What happened to Linda Evans?" And they were talking about the woman Linda Evans who was on *Dynasty*. But we're not talking about all of that—people had no idea.

Do you remember that? I'm not kidding you. [all laugh]

Because we would do that, if there was a big march. I mean, we would carry our big signs, *FREE LAURA WHITEHORN*, and women would come up to us and say, "Who's Laura Whitehorn? I've never heard of that person."

So, outside of the leftist circle, it wasn't like any of those people were household [names]. Silvia Baraldini was a household [name] in Italy. She was really well-known. Everyone knew who Silvia was because that government was trying to get her to move back there for ten years. Anyway, here in the US, it's an issue. Do you think, generalized, that the people really know who Assata Shakur is?

Judy: No.

Jay: They know Tupac.

Jane: Maybe I'm not being positive enough.

Penny: Well, when Assata wrote her book, it became a runaway bestseller, to everybody's amazement. It's really well-written, and it describes where they came from to do what they did, and that kind of thing. And she's still free, with a two-million-dollar price on her head.

These kinds of examples, and bringing people like her forward—like she brought herself forward to speak internationally—is major for exposing what the prison system is about and what it does to people.

Jane: Do you think that the women political prisoners are that visible, were that visible, to the generalized public?

Penny: I think the women political prisoners who did speak out led to the visibility. The women political prisoners led to the attention that we can get on the women prisoners now in California, like with California Coalition for Women Prisoners, who are doing so much activity around CIW (the Correctional Institution for Women).

Brooke: How do you think that happened?

Penny: Well, California Coalition for Women Prisoners has been doing political work for a very long time, led by women, many lesbians. They go to the legislature, they tug on coattails, pass out a lot of literature, and they stay very active.

Jane: The women political prisoners kept organizing. A lot of the work that Linda Evans did after she got out of prison, like being a cofounder of All of Us or None, and other work, was prisoner support and building the abolition movement. A lot of the women political prisoners, once they got out, they were organizing. And while they were inside, too. They did a lot of the AIDS activist work while they were inside, which happened on the East Coast and the West Coast, because they were in either DC or out here in Dublin, and it became nationally known.

That was very important. And then once they got out, they continued doing that work.

Penny: Absolutely.

Jay: The Dyke March publicized the issues of the women political prisoners. We tabled at Gay Day. I think we brought in people who heard about political prisoners at those tables. Some of them came into Out of Control. I think there were about twenty-five people through Out of Control over the years, and they came through us because of the organizing. Some of them have gone on to do work in other areas. But we organized them through our tabling at Gay Day and that kind of stuff.

Judy: Can I say, I think there's a political issue there, in terms of the early days, because when the work about women political prisoners started, there was a tension—let me put it that way—in the movement about "political prisoners" versus "social prisoners."

And the people who were doing social-prisoner work were not happy about a focus on political prisoners. Why was that? Because the women political prisoners weren't just smoking weed and getting caught, doing something minor that no one thinks should be punished. They were doing what we today call armed struggle. Weapons. Deliberate. And that was a politics not universally shared.

So, what appeared to be a division ultimately wasn't, but for a long while it appeared to be because some people disagreed with the underlying political basis of having that category of people called "political prisoners." I think nowadays nobody bothers with that distinction; those days are long gone. But back then, that was an issue.

Brooke: Do you remember how that debate happened?

Jane: Critical Resistance, the first big conference about the prison industrial complex took place in Berkeley; the organizing was led by Angela Davis. She was important in bringing us together. Ruth Wilson Gilmore and Rose Braz were also central to the organizing of the conference. Because Angela Davis had been in jail, and because she had been involved with the defense of George Jackson—when she used "prison industrial complex" language, she always brought up the political prisoners. She was one of the first people that did make that connection, and that brought the political prisoners up publicly.

Bo and I worked on the committee to organize the first Critical Resistance conference, and we were invited to do a workshop as Out of Control about the women political prisoners.

Judy: However, to this day, there is an issue. You go to a political event, and write me a postcard if they talk about political prisoners. I think more people know about it than talk about it at their events, but it still stays tamped down.

Jay: Well, I think that part of the issue was the fact that, also, we had to explain: why were these prisoners called "political prisoners"? It pushed us to explain that it was because of the politics behind their work, the conscious acts that they did. And so it was a dialogue that we had with ourselves, within our group, and in talking to people at our tables, we developed a politic about it through just doing the work.

MaestraPeace Mural, "Woman teacher of peace," 1994, on the San Francisco Women's Building. Foreground: Lolita Lebrón. Left to right: Alejandrina Torres, Norma Jean Croy, Marilyn Buck, Dylcia Pagán, and Susan Rosenberg. The background represents the thousands of women held in US prisons. The names of many women political prisoners are inscribed in the mural. Out of Control used the image in their outreach work.

But we did make connections between political prisoners and general prisoner issues. In *Out of Time*, we had social prisoners whom we worked with. One of our campaigns was Norma Jean Croy. She was a political prisoner in terms of this country, right? In the way that she was treated, and the time she got, being a Native woman. But she was actually a social prisoner. The acts that she did were not political acts. So we supported people that were considered social prisoners also. And we also sent the newsletter into the general prison.

Jane: We felt like, what Judy mentioned before about visibility and invisibility: that women prisoners are invisible, just like women political prisoners were invisible. So it was about all women prisoners. But if we weren't there, with a goal of putting out the word about women political prisoners, they wouldn't be mentioned. That includes the Puerto Rican women prisoners of war, too. I think more people knew about some of the men than they would about the women. Right?

Leonard Peltier. Geronimo Ji-Jaga Pratt. Geronimo's campaign was for everyone in California, in the state of California. And Mumia Abu-Jamal, certainly. So, if we weren't there, who would speak for the women? That was the quality of our commitment, was to raise the women political prisoners' names. And their stories.

MARILYN KALMAN, OUT OF CONTROL, AND "THE CODEFENDANTS"

Laura Whitehorn

In 1988, I was in the city jail in Washington, DC, in pretrial detention along with five codefendants—Marilyn Buck, Linda Evans, Susan Rosenberg, Alan Berkman, and Tim Blunk. We were not having a good time.

If you went to DC for any of the big antiwar demos in the '60s, you may be familiar with the DC Jail. The food is only borderline edible. The cells are cold and unclean (in every sense of the word). The jail is way overcrowded and noisy as hell. The guards range from bored to brutal. Fresh air is absent. And we were being held in "special conditions" due to the political nature of our case, which we named the "Resistance Conspiracy" case—an indictment for attacking symbols and institutions carrying out the US government's assault on humanity around the world and inside this country.

Our special conditions included relentless handcuffing/waist chaining/shackling, 23 ½ hour lockdown, lots and lots of nasty strip searches, and constant monitoring, all in addition to the regular, very ugly conditions visited upon all the other people incarcerated with us—almost all of whom, unlike us, were Black and Brown. The administration and guards referred to us as "the codefendants." They didn't say it with love.

Into this morass, in the summer of 1988, came Marilyn Kalman. Withdrawing a chunk of her less-than-hefty savings, she arrived, announcing that she, with her legal and organizational skills—and, thank the goddess, her good taste, generosity, and sense of humor—was temporarily closing her Bay Area practice and moving to DC for six months or more, to support us and, as it turned out, take care of us.

And she did. She visited regularly and whenever we needed her. She did research when needed, on legal matters but also on the scope of the political movement and whom we could or could not count on for support. She met with local DC activists and lawyers to get them to do whatever was needed, too.

Left to right: Marilyn "Mo" Kalman and Laura Whitehorn in the visiting room of FCI Dublin, California. Circa 1990.

And she worked some useful magic. At Passover in 1989, she convinced the administrator of the jail to allow her and another lawyer to bring in the makings of a seder. They submitted a memo listing what was needed; the administrator dutifully checked off the items permitted—boiled egg, YES; salt, matzoh, horseradish, parsley, all YES. He stamped DENIED next to the shank bone. He permitted haroseth—the sweet concoction of ingredients including nuts and honey. When it came to the ingredient sweet wine, the lawyers promised to replace that with grape juice.

But substitute they did not: It turns out Manischewitz wine smells sort of like grape juice, and armed with the signed memo from the administrator, the lawyers carried in all the makings for what should have been a seder but was, instead, an inebriated romp. Memorable and spirit-lifting, to say the least.

She brought us colored pencils—supposedly for doing legal work. She brought us books and cards. She brought us all sorts of "stationery" goods to brighten the bleak landscape we lived in.

She came to visit us at night when we were otherwise alone in our cells, insisting that she needed to see a few of us together. Because we were all separated in various "living" units, this was the only chance we had to hang out together, talk, and try to make sense of what had befallen our collective. She contacted our families when we couldn't. She befriended our friends.

She rallied support from people in DC and Maryland, especially working to gain backing from lesbian groups. She spoke on our behalf at a slew of political events, contacted media and handled annoying journalists, provided legal research and did whatever grunt work was required. I can't remember her ever saying no to a request from any of us.

On at least one occasion she saved a life. Alan was in the most fragile of health after debilitating chemotherapy treatment for a

Left to right, standing: Susan Goldberg; sitting: Marilyn "Mo" Kalman, Laura Whitehorn, Suzie Day in a restaurant in New York City after Laura Whitehorn was released from prison. Circa 2000.

second bout of cancer. When, late on a Friday night, we learned from incarcerated women working as orderlies in the infirmary that he was in danger of dying, one of us got to the phone on our block and called Kalman. She rushed to the jail for a late-night "legal visit" with Alan in the infirmary and was able to get him transferred to the hospital. He survived that incident and went on to live for another twenty years, the last fifteen in freedom.

After the case ended and we were all shipped to different federal prisons, she continued to visit. Marilyn, Linda, and I had the best of it, because we were in a California prison and Kalman was nearby. When I was released in 1999, it was to her house that I repaired, spending my first night with my love, Susie Day, in what Kalman and her equally generous and good-humored partner, her widow Susan Goldberg, turned into the "honeymoon suite." The next day, Kalman drove me to Oakland and sat in a car for eons while I visited with Yuri Kochiyama, who had recently been released from a medical facility.

Kalman did what was needed.

With the Out of Control crew, she made sure I had the things I needed for my first in-freedom apartment. I still cook with those pots and pans from Macy's—way better than I could have afforded just out of the gate.

I flew to California and visited Kalman and other OOC reprobates a few times after my release, slightly amazed at seeing you all in settings other than a prison visiting room. Kalman was always up for tooling around in her car with me, showing me the SF sights and of course eating dim sum till it came out of our ears. Susie and I came to the Bay Area for Kalman's—what, fiftieth—birthday bash, when we all gathered at a bar and she performed an entire cabaret act (including her unforgettable rendition of "Que Será, Será"), and she and Susan visited here in NYC a few times as well.

One of my favorite visits was the one Susie and I paid during the Dyke March one year. Finally, we could experience that huge, formidable gathering of formidable dykes, with Kalman managing things. She was very proud of her work building and organizing the Dyke March, and it was fabulous to be able to witness it firsthand.

Then, a few years ago—the year after Mo's death—at the much smaller (and less rambunctious) NYC Dyke March, I happened to talk to a young woman from SF who told me she'd been in the Dyke March organizing group out west. Did she know Marilyn Kalman, I of course asked? She gasped and we hugged and cried together as she told me how much Marilyn had taught her, how much she missed her, how the Dyke March would never be quite the same. That was a good cry.

I wish I could say I repaid Marilyn for all those years of generosity by helping to care for her in the last painful and difficult years of her life. She had a deep, loving community of support, but I only made it to the Bay Area to visit a few times and did little to help ease her last years. I am sorry for that. The best I can do to honor her amazing memory is to try to emulate her generosity, her willingness to support those more vulnerable, her stubborn refusal to let anyone need anything if she could provide it. But I doubt I'll ever measure up to Kalman in the days of the DC Jail Passover miracle.

Susan Goldberg and Mo Kalman took a road trip. This captures part of their trip: Mo on the ferry from Victoria, British Columbia, to Vancouver, British Columbia.

WOMAN DANCING
Laura Whitehorn

Graphic Credit: Laura Whitehorn, Courtesy Out of Control Collection

Laura is an accomplished artist and made this block print in 1998 while incarcerated at FCI Dublin, California.

THREE WOMEN MUSICIANS
Laura Whitehorn

Laura Whitehorn made this block print while incarcerated at FCI Dublin, California, in 1999.

SECTION 4: SPARKS FLY

Laura Whitehorn with two participants in the AIDS walkathon held inside FCI Marianna, Florida, to raise funds for HIV/AIDS work, circa 1990. It was one of the first prison walkathons in a women's facility to support HIV/AIDS community work on the outside. Of the approximately 99 women incarcerated in Marianna, 97 participated in the walkathon.

Photo Credit: Prison photo, Courtesy Laura Whitehorn

FIGHTING HIV/AIDS IN PRISON
Emily K. Hobson

"In our work, as in the work out there, collectively asserting life over death, humanity over prejudice and fear, creates power."[1] Writing these words to supporters in 1993, political prisoner Laura Whitehorn identified inside–outside solidarities as essential to the struggle against HIV/AIDS in prison. Across the 1980s and 1990s, AIDS activism by, for, and with people in prison fought both the epidemic and the carceral state. Women political prisoners and Out of Control played pivotal roles in mobilizing these struggles.

For many radicals of the era, HIV/AIDS became a primary lens for understanding and confronting the intertwined problems of imperialism, white supremacy, heterosexism, and incarceration. As Zoe Leonard, an artist and member of the AIDS Coalition to Unleash Power (ACT UP), put it, "What AIDS revealed was not the problem of the virus. What AIDS revealed was the problems of our society. It was this fissure through which everything, all the ways in which our society isn't working, became really clear."[2] This convergence of crises was starkly apparent inside prisons and jails. By the late 1980s, one in five people incarcerated in New York

---

1 Laura Whitehorn, "Collectively Asserting Life over Death Creates Power!" in *Voices from Inside: Prisoners Respond to the AIDS Crisis*, ed. ACT UP/San Francisco Prison Issues Committee (San Francisco: ACT UP San Francisco, 1993), 35–37. Prisons box, Whitehorn materials, Interference Archive (Brooklyn, NY). The essay is reprinted in Dan Berger and Emily K. Hobson, eds., *Remaking Radicalism: A Grassroots Documentary Reader of the United States, 1973–2001* (University of Georgia Press, 2020), 190–192.

2 Zoe Leonard as quoted in *United in Anger: A History of ACT UP* (directed by Jim Hubbard, 2012).

state were found to be HIV-positive on entering prison.[3] Initially, many activists viewed HIV/AIDS in prison primarily as an issue of transmission risk, due to prohibitions on condoms, clean needles, and the open expression of sexuality behind bars. Yet, in a pattern that remains true today, most people living with HIV/AIDS in prison became positive prior to incarceration. As many activists came to understand, poverty, racism, trauma, and a lack of health care and harm-reduction services heighten communities' vulnerability not only to criminalization and incarceration, but also to HIV.

One consequence of the racialized and classed history of HIV/AIDS is that women's prisons have seen the highest rates of the epidemic, even as men's prisons, being more numerous, hold the highest numbers. But this reality was obscured, and responses to it hampered, by a lack of recognition of AIDS in people assigned female at birth. Most women political prisoners went into prison already connected to feminist, queer, and community health movements, and were attentive to AIDS activism from early on. Susan Rosenberg, for example, had worked with Dr. Mutulu Shakur and other Black radicals who innovated the use of auricular acupuncture as a tool of heroin detox in Harlem and the Bronx. Still, Rosenberg recalls that she only fully understood the scale of the AIDS crisis when she saw how many sick and dying women filled the Washington, DC, jail. From there, she recognized that "the structural violence that resulted in genocidal death in the jail, or in the black community, or the failures of government to respond to the AIDS epidemic seemed to me to be part of a war against the marginalized of America."[4] Prisons—and especially

---

3 The Members of ACE Program (AIDS Counseling and Education) of the Bedford Hills Correctional Facility, *Breaking the Walls of Silence: AIDS and Women in a New York State Maximum-Security Prison* (Overlook Press, 1998), 19; New York State Department of Health AIDS Institute, *Focus on AIDS in New York State AIDS in Prison Project Fact Sheet* (April 1994), ed. Miki Conn (New York State Department of Health AIDS Institute, 1994), 3.

4 Susan Rosenberg, *An American Radical: Political Prisoner in My Own Country* (Citadel Press, 2011), 171.

women's prisons—pulled back a curtain on the scope and nature of the AIDS epidemic.

AIDS prison activism found key leadership among political prisoners and key expression through peer-education projects. The first such project began in New York state at the men's prison at Auburn, where Kuwasi Balagoon (1946–86)—a former Black Panther, anarchist, bisexual, and member of the Black Liberation Army (BLA)—died of AIDS. Grieving his death, Balagoon's codefendant David Gilbert and two fellow prisoners, Mujahid Farid (1949–2018) and Angel Nieves, joined together in 1987 to craft the Prisoner Education Project on AIDS (PEPA).[5] Participants included another BLA member and political prisoner, Albert "Nuh" Washington (1941–2000). The same year, and also in New York state, some two-dozen people at the women's prison Bedford Hills initiated AIDS Counseling and Education (ACE). Cofounders included two other codefendants of Gilbert and Balagoon, Kathy Boudin and Judy Clark, as well as Katrina Haslip (1959–92), formerly a kindergarten teacher in a Muslim school and then a law clerk in the prison library. When Haslip left Bedford Hills in 1990, she became a leader in the Change the Definition campaign, which pushed the Centers for Disease Control to expand the definition of AIDS to better address the epidemic in women, injection drug users, and poor people. She died of AIDS just weeks before the CDC implemented the expanded definition that would have registered her death among the epidemic's official toll. Other

---

[5] Mujahid Farid, "The Social Dimensions of AIDS in the Prisons" (unpublished essay, December 1989), in Gay Men's Health Crisis Records (Series X.A., Box 327, Folder 5), The New York Public Library (New York, NY), Astor, Lenox, and Tilden Foundations. See also David Gilbert, "The Struggle for Aids Education in Prison," *New Studies on the Left* 14, no. 1–2 (1989): 143–44; David Gilbert, interviewed and with a prologue by Dan Berger, "Grief and Organizing in the Face of Repression/The Fight against Aids in Prison," in *Rebellious Mourning: The Collective Work of Grief*, ed. Cindy Milstein (AK Press, 2017); and Esther Kaplan, "Organizing Inside," *Poz*, November 1, 1998, available online at https://www.poz.com/article/Organizing-Inside-1656-9407 (accessed March 27, 2021).

reverberations of ACE's work included a book by ACE members, a conference at Bedford Hills, a reentry project called ACE-OUT, and a documentary produced with videographers Catherine Saalfield and Debra Levine.[6]

PEPA and ACE were soon joined by similar projects around the United States, many of them also led by women political prisoners. Members of the Resistance Conspiracy case, including Marilyn Buck (1947–2010), Linda Evans, Susan Rosenberg, and Laura Whitehorn, and others including Dylcia Pagán, Alejandrina Torres, and Silvia Baraldini, worked to launch projects in Lexington prison (Kentucky), the Washington, DC, jail, FCI Marianna (Florida), FCI Dublin (California), and FCI Danbury (Connecticut). For its part, Out of Control informed outside supporters about AIDS prison activism, helped funnel HIV/AIDS information inside, and fueled efforts to pressure officials for a modicum of decent care and for compassionate release. Solidarity networks additionally grew through ACT UP prison committees in New York, Los Angeles, San Francisco, and Philadelphia, and through the efforts of Judy Greenspan in the ACLU National Prison Project, ACT UP San Francisco, and HIV in Prison Project.[7]

AIDS prison activists brought together practices of care work, advocacy, organizing, and political education. Each peer-education project started from a small cohort of people, some of whom were HIV-positive and others HIV-negative, but all of whom were affected by the losses of loved ones inside and outside the

---

[6] *Breaking the Walls of Silence,* 99–102. The film, which features Katrina Haslip and focuses on the work of ACE-OUT, is *I'm You, You're Me: Women Surviving Prisons, Living with AIDS* (directed by Debra Levine and Catherine Saalfield, 1992). It can be viewed online at https://vimeo.com/277354130 (accessed March 27, 2021).

[7] See also Queers United in Support of Political Prisoners (QUISP) with Linda Evans, Laura Whitehorn, and Susan Rosenberg, "Dykes and Fags Want to Know: Interview with Lesbian Political Prisoners" (1995), in *Let Freedom Ring: A Collection of Documents from the Movements to Free U.S. Political Prisoners,* ed. Matt Meyer (PM Press, 2008), 372–383.

Photo Credit: Prison photo Courtesy Linda Evans

Linda Evans (pictured here), while incarcerated at FCI Dublin, California, worked with PLACE, Pleasanton AIDS Counseling and Education. Twenty members of PLACE made two panels for the AIDS Memorial Quilt. One panel memorializes women who died in prison of AIDS and the other, shown here, children orphaned by AIDS. Circa 1989.

prison. They faced off against stigma and misinformation among peers and stark mistreatment from prison authorities. It proved common to see guards leaving sick people in cells for hours or days without assistance, denying people with HIV/AIDS their higher nutritional needs, or placing them in punitive segregation, not to mention a lack of qualified doctors and the denial of consistent or accurate medications. Illness and death were accelerated by jail and prison overcrowding and by the prevalence of tuberculosis, hepatitis C, and other infections to which people with HIV/AIDS are vulnerable. (By 1995, aspects of these problems began to be legally challenged through the class action lawsuit *Shumate v. California*.)

In the Washington, DC, jail, Resistance Conspiracy codefendants worked with other prisoners to issue demands to the administration and, after several months, were able to launch a project coordinated with the city's Whitman Walker Clinic. They continued similar work at FCI Marianna, where they measured success in such small changes as people's increased willingness to share a cell with a person living with HIV. By the early 1990s, at FCI Marianna, FCI Dublin (in Pleasanton AIDS Counseling and Education, or PLACE), and FCI Danbury, they implemented an extensive curriculum. Sessions ranged from introductory presentations for newcomers and guards to extended discussions of safer sex and safer drug practices, medical research and drug trials, alternative treatments, and the politics of race, gender, and class in the epidemic. Peer educators created bilingual materials in English and Spanish, carried out peer counseling, developed buddy programs for those who were sick, and led walkathons around the yard, through which prisoners donated precious commissary funds to local AIDS groups.[8]

While prison administrators tolerated some aspects of AIDS peer education, the work pushed boundaries. Discussions of HIV prevention raised the specters of homosexuality, contraband drug use, and sexual coercion or assault by guards. Peer educators helped others to file motions for treatment and early release. Even those efforts that appeared softest or most nonthreatening, such as the walkathons raising funds for children's AIDS care, could

---

8   For reflections on these tactics, see Emily K. Hobson with Rory Elliot, interview with Kathy Boudin, Linda Evans, and Crystal Mason, "Inside-Outside Organizing to Resist a Virus: Lessons from the AIDS Crisis for Our Fight During Covid-19," *The Abolitionist* 33 (Fall 2020), 4.

draw media attention and become means to publicize the lack of decent conditions and care inside.

AIDS peer-education projects were also tools of mourning, and several projects created quilt panels to honor the dead. The AIDS quilt at FCI Danbury took six months to make, involved seventy-seven women, and ultimately recognized 195 people who had died. Constructed to represent the prison itself, and to illustrate how grieving and resistance extended inside and beyond prison walls, the quilt included a plane flying a banner with the words of labor organizer Mother Jones—"pray for the dead and fight like hell for the living"—and a neatly stitched helicopter lowering a ladder near the prison fence. Grimly, laughably, or both, when first unveiled, the quilt produced near-panic among prison authorities, who feared its words and imagery coded concrete plans for escape.[9]

AIDS prison organizing revealed the lasting interrelationships between multiple radical movements, including Black, Puerto Rican, community health, feminist, and LGBTQ struggles. Its activists confronted a stigmatized and deadly epidemic catalyzed by the intersections of racism, sexism, and homophobia, and they shone a light on prisons as both political/economic and public health crises. The legacies of AIDS prison activism can be seen in many examples today. Just to name one of these, Laura Whitehorn and Mujahid Farid went on to form Release Aging People in Prison, which has fought hard against the New York state government's abandonment of people in prisons facing COVID-19.

The images of flight stitched onto the AIDS quilt at FCI Danbury remained merely metaphorical representations of escape. No one hovered outside the prison with a helicopter to help someone leap from a walkathon on the yard to freedom beyond the walls. Yet larger goals of liberation lay at the heart of work to contest HIV/

---

[9] Images of the quilt are held in the Susan Rosenberg papers, Sophia Smith Collection, Smith College.

AIDS in prisons and jails. In her 1993 call for "collectively asserting life over death," Laura Whitehorn hailed the solidarities connecting HIV/AIDS organizing inside and outside prison. At the same time, she named the stark differences that made it impossible for imprisoned people to simply mimic the tactics of others who could take to the streets to express their anger, grief, and rage. Rather, Whitehorn offered, outside activists could learn from the creativity and insights of people in prison who confronted HIV/AIDS. These activists' work showed that, somewhere in the future, defeating HIV/AIDS would demand not only compassionate release for a few, but a movement of abolition for all.

Photo Credit: Prison photo Courtesy Laura Whitehorn

While at FCI Marianna, Florida, Laura Whitehorn (pictured here), Marilyn Buck (pictured here) and Susan Rosenberg worked with the HIV/AIDS Counseling and Education group. This photo, circa 1994, features women incarcerated at FCI Marianna with a panel for the AIDS Memorial Quilt memorializing their family and friends who died with AIDS. The panel was presented to Big Bend Cares, an outside organization, at a World AIDS Day event inside the prison.

RESISTANCE RISES FROM THE ASHES
Kate Raphael

In late February 1991, Stephen Fish, a friend from the AIDS Coalition to Unleash Power (ACT UP) and Stop AIDS Now or Else, died of AIDS. Once his mother had gone back to Iowa, and his ashes were in a ceramic container on my mantel, it was time to face what I had put off as long as possible: cleaning out his apartment. I went there with a couple other members of LAGAI, Lesbians and Gays Against Intervention.[1]

Stephen was a pretty typical San Francisco white gay man in his early forties. He came from a working-class Baptist family, had made it out of Iowa and graduated from college (even getting a master's in divinity before breaking with the church). In college in South Dakota, he supported the Black freedom movement and marched against the Vietnam War. He migrated to San Francisco by way of Minneapolis, got active in the Radical Faeries, and became cochair of Black and White Men Together. When he tested positive for HIV, he threw himself into AIDS activism, helping to found PISD, People with Immune System Disorders. We were both word processors at big corporate law firms, but when he was diagnosed with AIDS, he quit work, saying that working for the Man when you didn't have to was stealing from yourself and your community. He was stubborn and quietly hilarious. A newspaper article about AIDS activists in the summer of 1989 called him "elfin."

Like so many gay men of his era, he had awesome taste in clothes and furniture. After separating out the useful papers and donating them to the GLBT Historical Society, packing up the

---

[1] Originally "Lesbians and Gays Against Intervention in Central America," now, after several updates, LAGAI—Queer Insurrection.

photos and buttons to display at the memorial, we started to wonder what to do with the antique marble-top nightstand, cute kitchen cart, not to mention the basket of perfectly preserved stuffed animals.[2]

I don't remember who came up with the idea of a garage sale, but Mark Wang and Sandy Mack, both also now dead of AIDS, who produced the edgy radical queer community TV show *Electric City*, offered the front yard of their house on Collingwood, just a block from the epicenter of gay political culture.[3] We decided to hold it the first weekend of June (Pride month) as a fundraiser for the Women Political Prisoner Commissary Fund, a project LAGAI cofounded in 1990 with Out of Control: Lesbian Committee to Support Women Political Prisoners. With the contents of Stephen's household as the cornerstone, we put out a call for donations and soon had a yard full of clothes, toys, books, furniture, which translated into over $1,000 to keep women prisoners in tampons, shampoo, stamps, and snack food. A tradition was born.

Those first few years, there was sadly no shortage of stuff to be gleaned from the possessions of fellow AIDS activists. In 1993, Joan Kaye, a member of LAGAI, died suddenly of a stroke at age fifty-one. Like Stephen, Joan had been an activist from the mid-sixties straight through to the day she died, but her coming out had been harder. She grew up in New York, but her father died when she was in high school and she moved to Florida, where she started college at the University of Florida. This was the early sixties, and the range of acceptable behavior for women was very narrow. Joan and a woman friend were kicked out of school because someone thought their relationship was too close. She and a friend drove to San Francisco and Joan went to work at the post office, where she

---

2   See the Stephen Fish papers at the GLBT Historical Society, https://oac.cdlib.org/findaid/ark:/13030/c83r0tg7/.

3   A clip of *Electric City* can be found at https://www.youtube.com/watch?v=_J4Ejcan9m8 (accessed February 3, 2022).

became passionately involved in the union. For much of the eighties and nineties, she had the absolute worst job for a union member—validating time sheets so the workers could get paid. There were a million rules, none of them intended to help the workers, and Joan was always getting in conflict with management. A few months before she died, she got a job she liked much better: helping people make sure their bulk mailings were done right. Since she was now interacting with the public, she started dressing up for work, and Joan LOVED dressing up. She loved bright-colored clothes and sparkly jewelry, and had a bit of a shopping addiction. So when she died, and we went to clean out the apartment where she had lived for several decades, we found blouses still in the bags and dresses with the tags still on, political T-shirts dating back to the Nixon administration, and racks and racks of earrings. She died in May, just after the 1993 March on Washington and just in time for the political prisoners' garage sale.

Political Prisoners and Queer International Solidarity

LAGAI was born in 1983 as successor to the gay and lesbian caucus of a coalition to pass a San Francisco resolution to end US aid to the right-wing government of El Salvador. An early campaign of the LGBT solidarity community involved collecting hundreds of cardboard milk cartons, to which we affixed pictures of resisters who had been "disappeared" by the Salvadoran military—an homage to mainstream milk-carton campaigns displaying pictures of missing US children. After a short rally we carted the milk cartons to the post office in wheelbarrows and mailed them to the State Department, demanding they stop funding the Salvadoran death squads and help locate the disappeared activists. (Incidentally, such an action involves dealing with a lot of sour milk, and we don't necessarily recommend it.)

Although LAGAI's early focus was solidarity with the revolutionary movements in Latin America, its politics have always been broadly internationalist and anti-imperialist. After the First Intifada (Uprising) broke out in 1987, we joined campaigns to free the more than 75,000 Palestinians taken prisoner by the Israeli government between 1987 and 1993; some of those campaigns were initiated by the Israeli organization Women for Women Political Prisoners. We supported Irish queers in Boston who were demanding to march in the St. Patrick's Day Parade, and through them we learned about the struggles for recognition of the IRA women freedom fighters in the H Block/Armagh prison, who were less well-known internationally than the male hunger strikers.

Left to right: Kate Raphael and Julie Starobin holding a banner at a demonstration in support of returning Italian national, anti-imperialist political prisoner Silvia Baraldini home to Italy. After a ten-year campaign, the United States transferred Silvia to an Italian prison. Circa 1991.

Though we ardently oppose US attacks on Cuba, some of us had helped welcome the Bay Area queers who left Cuba on the 1980 Mariel boatlift, many of whom had been imprisoned for being queer. When Cuba announced mandatory quarantine of people with HIV/AIDS in 1986, we struggled with so-called "leftists" who refused to condemn this policy in Cuba at the same time we were fighting to defeat the AIDS quarantine initiative placed on the California ballot by Lyndon LaRouche. Our position is, was, and always will be: no criminalization of queerness or disability, anywhere.

Supporting political prisoners has always been viscerally important to everyone in LAGAI. Some of us had relatives in prison, some had had family members persecuted during the McCarthy era, others had been forced into exile from Argentina or Chile. At least one LAGAI cofounder had been a draft resister during the Vietnam war; another narrowly escaped prosecution for being queer while in the navy in the 1980s. Older LAGAI members had belonged to Black Panther support committees, organizing to Free Huey, Free Bobby and Ericka, Free Angela and All Political Prisoners. Some had worked with Lesbians Against Police Violence, which organized in San Francisco in the early 1980s, highlighting the way in which San Francisco police occupied the largely Latinx Mission district much as US-trained and -funded troops were occupying Latin American countries.

Some of us have been imprisoned because of our activism, and all of us know that we could be. One of our members, Deeg, called the political prisoners' commissary fund "Invest in Your Future," because one day you might need this fund yourself. We all understand that a movement that doesn't take care of its people inside is one that can't survive and doesn't deserve to survive.

Come Out, Get Out, Let Everyone Out!

In June 1988, we published the first issue of a newsletter called *Out!* It was a play on both "US Out!," the rallying cry of the anti-intervention movements, and the radical queer chant "Out of the Closets and Into the Streets!" The second issue of *Out* had an article about the success of the lawsuit challenging the Lexington Control Unit, the torture center where three women political prisoners were being held, as well as a cover article about resisting grand juries (titled "What Not to Do with Your Mouth"). The third issue led with an article about two California ballot initiatives that would have led to increased criminalization of people who had or were suspected of having HIV, including prisoners and sex workers. As repression escalated during the Reagan and Bush years, we had to make sure we had at least one article in each issue that was *not* about police raids, executions, or new ways to put people in prison.

A year after we started *Out*, Out of Control decided to start a newsletter focusing on prisoners, especially women prisoners. Some LAGAI members were also members of OOC—Deeg, in fact, came up with the name Out of Control—and we agreed to send their newsletter, *Out of Time*, along with *Out*, to our mailing list of about 500 people, which included a few dozen prisoners. When we switched from a xeroxed 8.5 × 14-inch newsletter to an eight-page newspaper, renamed *UltraViolet* (the invisible fringe of the rainbow), *Out of Time* became the centerfold. When *Out of Time* stopped publishing, OOC sent an introductory copy of *UltraViolet* to everyone on their mailing list, with instructions on how to subscribe.

With the rise of the internet, fewer activists outside want to get newspapers in the mail. But queer prisoners can't get enough materials that are free, interesting, sometimes even funny, and that cover issues relevant to their lives. Though we continue to table at book fairs and other events (when it isn't COVID times), almost three-quarters of the 3,300 people who get *UltraViolet* now are in prisons or jails around the country. Since 2015 every issue has included prisoner writings. Prisoners write about conditions in their prisons, what it's like to be queer in prison, daily struggles, their hopes for the future, organizing they're doing or want to do, and their thoughts on everything going on in the country. Sometimes prisoners in different prisons communicate with each other by responding to articles in our pages.

Nearly all the prisoners who receive and contribute to *UltraViolet* are queer and/or trans. They are from all over the country, many nationalities and races and genders, with a broad spectrum of politics. Few of them are "political prisoners" in any orthodox sense. They are in prison because of racism and poverty, sexism and heterosexism and anti-trans laws, criminalization of sex work and drugs. But we also know, and they know, that all of those issues are political, and insisting on living as a queer person inside prison walls is a powerful form of resistance.

LAGAI (Lesbians and Gays Against Intervention) and Out of Control tabling at Gay Pride. Circa 1989. Left to right, back: Chaya Gordon, Deeg Gold, Jay Mullins, Mary Carol Randall, Julie Starobin (behind banner), Daniel Ward. Front: Deni Asnis, Blue Murov, Jane Segal, Tom Reynolds.

NOTE

Debbie Africa

June 16, 2021

Several months ago, I was asked if I remember an organization called "Out of Control" that supported the MOVE women at Muncy in the time we were there (1981–95). I could not and had to think about it, since it's been a long time, and much has happened since.

Debbie Africa spent almost forty years in prison. In 2018 she was released. This photo is Debbie after her release.

Photo Credit: Joe Piette
Courtesy Joe Piette

When Noelle said the name "Jane Segal," though—yes! I then remembered—"Yes," I said. I remembered the name Jane Segal . . . as I reminisced about the hardship of prison life during that time for us, what jumped out at me were the unexpected large donations we received for commissary items around Christmas for a few years, and the ongoing correspondence that followed.

I cannot remember exact dates, but I surely know that there were many people who spoke out against the injustices of the prison conditions, and "Sparks Fly" is a name I recognize as one.

In the years we received donations for commissary items from Sparks Fly—this was huge for me personally, because I had young children at home that other family members were caring for—it freed up some support that enabled me to feel more at liberty to share with others what I had received unsolicited, as a gift, and appreciated very much.

The male-guards-on-female-inmates "pat search" letters to the Muncy administration were even bigger, because as we all know the immoral written policy was such an egregious violation of our persons it made some women feel shamed in talking, let alone protesting, about it—but not MOVE, and not Sparks Fly, just to name a couple. This was even more appreciated, by our families and other supporters as well. It was a unified effort involving all supporters looking for a reason to fight.

The letters of support and correspondence, from Sparks Fly among other organizations, were great. I loved them because they kept my mind centered on working, lending my knowledge and experience to others in need of guidance or assistance, and less on the things I had no control over and could not change.

The connections with these movements ended up being enduring relationships, because whatever background, walk of life, race, ethnicity, gender, religion any of us came from—and they were all different—we all had one thing in common: fighting injustice, and it's what we did. That was the common denominator: the goal of justice.

Finally, in June 2018, I was released from prison (Cambridge Springs) after almost forty years, and the reunification with my family was TERRIFIC! Mike Jr., aided by attorney Brad Thomson, pulled up the rear of the four decades of hard work and struggle that culminated into my release—my husband, Mike Sr., was released four months later, and the rest of the MOVE 9 followed.

Appreciative of all the work and support that paid off. There are still challenges I face, of course, that are paramount, but I advocate for prioritizing your children no matter what fight you're in, or what organization you belong to; our children need us first.

Thanks for this opportunity.

Sincerely,
Debbie

Photo Credit: Prison photo
Courtesy: Out of Control Collection

Left to right, top row: Debbie Sims Africa, Consuewella Dotson Africa, Janine Phillips Africa, Merle Austin Africa. Bottom row: Ramona Africa, Sue Leon Africa, Janet Holloway Africa. The Africas were members of the MOVE organization that was firebombed by the City of Philadelphia in 1985. These women served decades in prison.
The last of the MOVE prisoners were released in 2020.

EVERYONE COMES FROM SOMEWHERE
Noelle Hanrahan

As a young butch lesbian in San Francisco in the late 1980s, I was searching for ways to challenge the state. The women in Out of Control were cute, funny, dynamic, and provided one hell of a political compass. I would see them everywhere.

The connections they shared with the revolutionary women inside prison, I knew, had everything do with our and my own liberation. They were also dykes who dove right into the national work and held other revolutionaries accountable without apology. I was one of a generation inspired by their presence, tactics, and newsletter.

I was only on their periphery, but that was exactly the point.

Out of Control shaped the entire culture by their presence, transforming public space and consciousness. Questions and demands were visible on the streets, in community newspapers, and in dozens of local lesbian community spaces like Old Wives Tales.

I would not have begun recording the voices of prisoners had I not met and been moved by Jennifer Beach, Jay Mullins, Jane Segal, Julie Starobin, Blue Murov, rita bo brown, Mo Kalman.

I gained a sense of possibility. It was not exactly permission, but more that the path had been worn. I felt a sense of place. Because of their presence, I knew that lesbian revolutionaries can and should work directly for and with Mumia Abu-Jamal. I knew I was focused on exposing neocolonialism through prison work, but while doing that I felt I could take my whole lesbian self with me.

Lesbians supported the liberation of Assata. What is not to LOVE about that.

As a white working-class lesbian, I was inspired to negotiate the artificially constructed colonial divisions and not let them deter my revolutionary work.

Out of Control taught me how to begin to bridge race, class, and gender boundaries. They also taught me that you had to come to the work with a profound respect and the willingness to listen and learn. The magic of Prison Radio is that it amplifies self-determination and autonomy. There are so many times in political work when you are working across race, age, class, culture divides where you may not understand something that is happening, but you must be humble, quiet, and patient with yourself. You have to be uncomfortable and listen, because it is very likely something that we need to learn, or meet in a way that is respectful of the space that other people are in.

GOING INTO THE PRISON

Chrystos

For Linda Evans

the guard growls, What's this?!
Poetry, I answer, just Poetry
He waves me through
with a yawn
that delights me
So I smuggle my words in
to the women
who bite them chewing starving
I'm honored to serve them
bring color Music Feelings
into that soul death
Smiling as I weep
for Poetry who has such a bad reputation
She's boring, unnecessary, incomprehensible
obscure, effete
The perfect weapon
for this sneaky old war horse
to make a rich repast of revolution

CELL PORTRAIT

Laura Whitehorn

Block print by Laura Whitehorn while she was incarcerated at FCI Dublin.

HISTORY MAKES HER OWN HEROES: A REMEMBERANCE OF SALLY MILLER GEARHEART

By Lani Ka'ahumanu

Born April 15, 1931 ~ Pearisburg, VA
Died July 14, 2021 ~ Ukiah, CA
Lesbian Feminist Separatist
Educator Activist Author Orator Scholar Visionary
"...and fun beyond measure."

I met Professor "Just call me Sally" Gearhart in a Basic Feminism 101 class at San Francisco State in 1976, the year the Women Studies [WOMS] BA program was launched. She the lesbian feminist separatist, and her co-teacher Mina Caufield a communist feminist, a heterosexual married mother of five children, eloquently taught/discussed their view of feminism, patriarchy, sex, race, and class all while modeling respect and love for one another.

Sitting halfway up the stairs in the auditorium-style classroom I watched women of all ages come in looking for a familiar face and a seat. The room was buzzing. Many of us, including me, were out or coming out as lesbians. We were woman-identified women loving women. Some of us were womyn loving wimmin. Women's music and culture were flourishing in the Bay Area. There were women's concerts and dances. Olivia Records was producing women's music albums. We were "filling up and spilling over" with Cris Williamson and Meg, Margie, Holly, Linda, Mary, Theresa, and Sugar Mama Gwen Avery, and poets Pat Parker and Judy Grahn and so many others. There was the Full Moon Café with a little feminist bookstore tucked inside the long narrow room under the stairs to the upper floor. Tee Corinne signed two of her Cunt Coloring Books there for me. One, a gift for my daughter. Old Wives Tales and A Woman's Place Book Stores, Artemis Society and the bars and places to dance—Peg's, Maude's, Scott's and A Little More to name a few were hopping. I'd taken Women and Madness the previous semester, but none of this had prepared me for Sally's lecture.

TYRANNY IN THE DELIVERY ROOM

Sally
Preacher of the hour
Loving every minute of her time with us
Poised and self-assured
Breaking down the patriarchy
Pink and blue
Dolls and trucks
Sex roles
Sexism
Tomgirls and sissies
Heterosexism
Marriage motherhood
Men's control of women's bodies
Women's lives
Violence
She had the whole class in her hands
and held us asking
Who are we separate from men?

Her deep expressive voice
Matched her dramatic physical gestures and facial expressions
Her large hands emphasizing each point

She came for the patriarchy again from another direction
broke it down and put it back together
It's not like I hadn't heard some of this before
It was her full-bodied passion

                    and awe-inspiring performance
                sparking the possibility, NO the probability
                of a lesbian feminist separatist revolution
                            Nothing would stop us
                                I heard the call
                        I was ready to run down the aisle
                    She was the role model I was looking for

♀ ♀ ♀

In the summer of 1974, two years before I met Sally, I had moved two miles away from my children and husband. I was then thirty-one years old. I'd been married eleven years to my high school sweetheart whom I met a few weeks after my sixteenth birthday. I had been taking business courses in high school so I would be able to find a job in case my husband died and I was left to raise the children. Three and a half years later in 1963, I married my steady beau the captain of the football team. My life path was now set or so I thought.

By the late sixties I was a fulltime suburban housewife and mother. My husband taught at the high school where we met. I was a volunteer mom at the elementary school: recess lady, field trip driver, art corner projects, and ice cream lady on Friday's. I was Another Mother for Peace, marched against the Viet Nam war, supported Cesar Chavez UFW organizing efforts and brought groceries for the Black Panther free breakfast program. I had begun taking one class a semester at the community college. I remember thinking I'd done it all.

I paid close attention to feminist authors appearing on the talk shows. Feminism began making sense. Much to my extended family's dismay and embarrassment I dropped Mrs. and claimed Ms. This branded me a feminist.

In the early '70s I started crying for no apparent reason. I was struggling and couldn't figure out what was wrong. One day my husband, and old friend told me he'd figured out why I'd been crying. "You've never had a life of your own. You need to leave. I'll take the children; you can't do what you need to do if they're with you." As soon as I heard it, I knew he was right. We'd grown up to be very different people. I moved to a studio apartment near the school in July 1974. We did our best to take care of our children and each other although separated by two miles and two worlds.

That fall I was hired as a teacher's aide at my kids' school. For the first time in my life, I had a paying job, and was living on my own. I was excited to find out who I was, and what I wanted to do with my life. I was single. The last time I was single I was sixteen. I had no desire or need to date or couple. I had lots of exploring and growing up to do. Leaving my children was [and still is] the hardest thing I've ever done. I never looked back and cried myself to sleep for months.

At the end of the school year, I moved from the San Mateo suburbs to an apartment in the city and transferred to San Francisco State University. I took the plunge and for the first time registered as a fulltime student majoring in Psychology. I worked as a waitress in a fancy restaurant and was coming out as a lesbian to everyone including my children and family.

For me
Sally was a Lesbian Feminist Separatist Rock Star
who made sense out of my life
concepts and language
gave me permission
encouraged me
to be
unapologetically
my self
a woman
Separate from the roles, the rules and
the assumed selflessness

I switched my major to Women Studies

        Sally was an action figure
        I wanted to be her
        I wanted to be like her
        She was my hero and guide
        12 years older than me
        She was like a sister
        And in time my cherished mentor

We became friends when we served on the Women Studies Hiring Committee. I was one of the student reps. We had long meetings, dynamite discussions after reading vitae, deciding whom we'd interview for proposed classes, setting up interviews, interviewing, deciding whom to hire and who would make the calls.

We always snacked or ate lunch. Sally with her soft white bread, a can of potted meat, peanuts in their shells and a couple Pepsis. She was disgusted with my healthy food sprinkled with roasted sunflower seeds. We were jokingly "grossed out" with each other's food and beverage choices. I mean there's not many things grosser than potted meat. [*Potted meat is a greyish brown paste of ground left over animal parts – beef, chicken, pig, organs etc. It looks sort of like liverwurst only whipped to a thick spread-able paste. It comes in a small cat food type can with a little ring you pull to open. She loved it and would moan it was so good.*]

Sally invited me to come up to Women's Land in Willits. She and several other lesbians had purchased property and were creating a women's community to explore what it meant to live as free of the constraints of patriarchy as possible. I arrived in my VW bus. There she was forty feet away swinging an ax, splitting logs for her wood stove. Wearing black jeans, and bare breasted she was breathtakingly gorgeous. She left the ax in the log, waved, and came to greet me with a big smile and long hug. We walked around the land talking. She was excitedly working on *Wanderground:*

The Stories of Hill Women, a Science Fiction novel. She stopped suddenly and said, "Oh, I've got to show you something." She led us into a wooded area where a small silver Airstream travel trailer camper stood. She proudly opened the door to show me her Pepsi stash. The camper was filled with cases of Pepsi top to bottom and right to the trailer door's edge. Her relationship with Pepsi was legendary.

Back in 1973 Sally was the first out lesbian in the country to be offered a tenure-track position. Academics and activism were not a favorable mix. She put her tenure on the line in 1978 when she and Harvey Milk led the successful fight against the Proposition 6 Briggs ballot Initiative. Prop 6 would have banned homosexuals from teaching in California schools. She and Harvey were the perfect pair. Both BIG-personality-one-of-a-kind charismatic characters who were media savvy, articulate, pioneers aware of their time and place in history and going for it. They shared similar feminist politics, a clown's sense of humor, and a comic's perfectly timed delivery. The demands of the campaign were intense. While those of us on the ground spread out across the state knocking on doors talking with people about No on 6, she and Harvey handled media interviews, rally speeches, appearances, etc.

This whole time Sally was teaching her classes. One afternoon I met up with Sally and her lover Jane Gurko a professor and my advisor. We sat down in Sally's office. Sally bent over, forearms on her knees, head down. She was exhausted, "didn't feel right" "felt lost". I said I thought after so many appearances she had become the character "Sally Gearhart" sort of a caricature of herself and lost her self along the way. She was out of balance, off center. Jane blurted "That's it!" Sally agreed and felt some relief.

The campaign was closing in on election day. Harvey called Sally the night they were debating State Representative John Briggs author of Prop 6 on live statewide TV. Harvey wanted to know what earrings he should wear. She laughed, "Oh why not dangling?" And they took off from there. Their shared humor, amity, and respect for one other grounded the pre-debate tension. Sally was a master debater. They were ready for Briggs. Briggs however was nowhere ready for a lesbian and gay man who couldn't be intimidated or shamed and who were primed to debate him.

Three weeks later Harvey and Mayor George Moscone were assassinated in City Hall by former Supervisor Dan White. The whole city came to the Castro, and we walked with candles silently down Market Street to City Hall. Sally spoke at Harvey's memorial. Over the years, Sally told me this story a couple times.

Near the end of her life, on different occasions Sally asked, "Why did Diane Feinstein call me?" I would respond, the Mayor called you the afternoon she was to announce the Dan White verdict. She wanted to talk with you before she spoke with the media. She said, "Your community is about to explode. Get yourself down here." The jury had not found Dan White guilty of first-degree murder as originally charged. They found him guilty of voluntary manslaughter the weakest conviction possible for his horrific actions. Mayor Feinstein called you because you and Harvey were respected leaders of our community. She wanted to talk with you as a leader, as a peer, as a strategist about ways to handle the situation, save her from mutiny, and save her reputation as Mayor. White Night riots that exploded when Diane made the announcement stunning the city, especially our community. I was at the riot. You felt you were put in an awkward position being "inside city hall" rather than in the streets with the community but you understood the position she was in and did what you could to assist. *"YES, yes that's right, thank you, that's right."*

After eleven years I graduated in 1979 with a BA in Women Studies. I was the first person in my family to earn a college degree. I was burned out, needed a break, attended the March on Washington for Lesbian and Gay Rights, and left the city.

Eighteen months later when I returned to my beloved San Francisco lesbian community, to my family of friends I knew what was in store for me – a lesbian who in the interim had fallen in love with a man. A lesbian who was coming out as a lesbian identified bisexual to clarify where I would be standing if the shit hit the fan. This coming out identity also assuaged my internalized biphobia and sense of loss. The harsh personal attacks, public humiliations and shunning stunned me. I met with Sally. She asked, "Is it true–you're bisexual?" I told her I was, and nothing had changed, not my woman centered identity, not my feminist politics, and not where I'd be putting my energy. Sally I'm the same woman. I'm not going any where and I won't be kicked out. She heard what I was saying, saw I was happy, loved me, and wanted to understand but she didn't. She needed time to think about it. She hung in there, asked me hard questions, and listened. I asked, "Why is my personal not political?" Sally never doubted me. We trusted each other. We stayed in touch. I sent her the bisexual articles I published in PLEXUS the Bay Area women's newspaper, Coming UP! a lesbian and gay weekly [now Bay Times], the SF Pride Parade magazine and the 1987 Lesbian and Gay March on Washington Civil Disobedience Handbook "Are we visible yet?". Sally told me I was just hitting my stride. She loved me.

Loraine Hutchins' and my anthology, *BI ANY OTHER NAME: Bisexual People Speak Out* (Alyson, 1991) was garnering rave reviews, flying off the shelves and heading towards its third printing. The book catapulted both Loraine and me into the national spotlight. The book also rode the rising tide of the national bisexual movement.

email exchange
5.21.91

Sally
How do we balance the token, the pioneer, the pedestal with the struggle to be truly free our selves inside ourselves, and with others?

How do we learn to be graceful and gracious?
How do we spark and shine publicly
without being seen as conceited and full of ourselves?

Oh sweetheart, remember this is all a dance, all the same thing. You remember by asking.

It is a balance, yes, but you know already that love is what is happening to you.

You know when you're embracing love and when you're not.

I've seen you for years now. You're already doing it and someday you'll believe it.

I'm beginning to believe it and the authentic moments are more and more frequent for me. Trust your loving self. We can reflect ourselves back and forth to each other until it's clear that there's only one, and love is.

Journal entry post call.
thursday night july 25, 1991
6 pm ish
Sally calls
leaving me a message
I can hear her voice
on my machine
I run down the hall
to say hello
to say oh Sally
how are you
we laugh
she asks
how are you doing
in your hero stage?
are you enjoying it?
is it fun?
she of course
is moving into her

sage period
she says she's not quite there yet
it's not something you get
she says it will come over her
she doesn't know
if she's ready
if she's good enough
I say SALLY you are totally good enough
okay she says
we are both ready
you the hero
me the sage

her voice filling me
with love, esteem,
inspiration, confidence
she is proud of me
and appreciates how far I've come
I say
it's exciting
it's a busy time
it means 14 messages on my answering machine
she laughs, welcome to the fold
oh don't I know that one
you are in your hero stage
aren't you?
it has taken me two years
to phase out all speaking commitments

I say,
it takes that long?

yes, she says
yes, listen to this Lani

NO, listen to the NOOOOOO
doesn't it resonate?
NOOOOOOOOOO
or
just let me think about it
or
if you reach the bottom of the barrel
she laughs, that deep rich laugh
I have only one more panel
to be part of
and that is it
it has taken two years
to pull away

she gives me her new phone number
I wonder, do you have a machine?
yes, but even on busy days
there are only 2-3 messages

she tells me to hold out
for the job I want
don't be a secretary
don't do it
she will put energy out
for a paid activist job

1992 email - I asked about accessible leadership and leading with an open heart without burning out. She counseled

"Take time for yourself at least once a week, an afternoon, or an hour a day and realize every day you have a choice to stop everything and go to a Buddhist monastery. Remember you're doing what you're doing because you love to do it. I was a very accessible

leader. I tried several times to limit that or "protect" myself, but it never worked."

1995 email exchange

Oh Sally
I'm stuck.
I know the speech is written
Waiting for me to open,
and catch as it falls
into my lap (top)
The words come and go
But mostly go right by me
My vessel isn't ready
My channel not clear
I catch glimpses
Exciting at times
Only to arrive at a dead end
Although some worthy sentences
Are written the whole is useless

Lani honey
This is so painful I can hardly stand it.
I can't think of many worse places to be.
It's why I'm taking theater improv classes, to stop thinking
thinking sinks my ship every time
I'm learning how to trust the moment,
trust that everything I've done my whole life through
up until this moment
will come to me when the time is ready.
And still I worry,
worry that I'll just make a flying fool of myself in front of all of them.
And so I think some more.

When, on rare occasions, I have been able to let go, it all has indeed come,
and in plenty of time for me to get it set in my head.
But those times are so rare.
More often I've just kept worrying and trying and crying and crying.
And yes, I've gotten through it and it was okay.
But here is a little true thing, my Lani: in the past ten years I've given maybe a total of six public speeches and five of them were disasters for me
(though they were well-received)
because I was doing it the old way.
I know the new way is just a whisper away
but I'm not good at trusting it yet.
Only once was I there, really there.
I wish I had an "answer" to all this.
One that I could articulate.

My life took off. I didn't see Sally for several years. We emailed and called each other occasionally. When I finally had some real down time, I made my way up to Willits. It was a very hot day. The sun was intense. Sally loved the sun. We sat naked, she in full sun while I was just a few feet away sitting on a chair under an umbrella in the shade. What a gift, we had lazy time to catch up. We talked about the latest happenings in her Willits community and the Bay Area, the HIVAIDS safer sex education work I was doing, and the shifting paradigms, when she noticed me glance down there, Sally immediately pointed to her vulva and declared, "Them's not gray hairs honey, they're cobwebs!" We started screaming and laughing hysterically, that was a good one Sally! I thought we'd pee our chairs! We laughed every time we told that story.

I don't remember who or exactly when someone told me Sally had Alzheimer's, but two days later we were sitting across from one another laughing and catching up like we'd always done regardless of how long it had been since the last time we'd heard from or seen each other. At eigthy-five she was as energetic, and sure-footed as ever. She asked about my life, my son, and writing and began to stretch her body. One leg slowly moved straight up above her head, her arm stretched up and her fingers curved, lightly over the bottom of her foot for a 1,2,3,4,5... moment and the leg came down. Her other leg, arm, and hand moved straight up stretching until stretching was completed. She did this effortlessly without missing a beat in our conversation. Her grace and flexibility always astonished me.

Sally asked me to visit again; we made another date. I never mentioned Alzheimer's and I never felt the need to bring it up. I left that one to her.

On the three-hour drive home, I thought about visiting her one weekend a month. I wanted to be there with her. I would be an Alzdoula for her journey. I'd never heard of such a thing but losing your memory is a form of dying separate from your body dying. You're aware of losing your awareness. I would want a safe place to think/talk about all that if I needed to, I would want a safe place to be my self even as I was forgetting who I was, I would want a safe place to let go and be who I was becoming, I would want a safe place with someone who shared lived memories with me and never got tired of hearing me ask or tell. I would want the safety and comfort of an old friend who held a joyful positive space filled with the possibility of laughter at any moment, who could look me in the eye without sadness, or fear, or grief, or pity, or drama, and love me.

Three weeks later, on my next visit we had easy fun. I never tired of her reciting poetry. We sang. We played Chinese checkers. We talked about my memoir. The time passed quickly. She asked when I could return. I told her I wanted to visit one weekend a month. I'd arrive on the late side of Saturday morning and leave Sunday early afternoon. She looked at me, "For how long?" Meeting her eyes, "For as long as you're here. It's an honor and a blessing to accompany you." She thanked me. "I love you Sally Miller Gearhart." "I love you Lani Ka'ahumanu." This was the only time around me she ever gave a nod to her illness.

We both looked forward to our monthly time together. Sally defined the time, the pace and space we shared. Her favorite sing-along songs included "Seventy-Six" Trombones from *Music Man*. I'd sing the first verse with her, and she'd carry on singing all the verses with great gusto. I wondered aloud if she ever played a musical instrument. With a sense of pride she replied, "I was first trombone in high school and in college." Another delightful surprise. We'd also sing ... Bing Crosby's *Would you like to swing on a star, carry moonbeams home in a jar and be better off than you are, or would you rather be a mule...* I was happy to be her back-up singer. When we discovered we both took tap dance as children, we jumped up and Shuffle(d) Off To Buffalo! I kept thinking if I was the new kid at school, I'd want to be friends with Sally, especially on the playground. She'd know what was happening because she was what was happening.

Come lunch time there was always the predictable commentary on the green food I brought to eat and my pro-biotic drinks. She enjoyed a bowl of buttery mashed potatoes, covered in melted cheddar cheese with a couple slices of crisp bacon on top or a rare random frozen macaroni and cheese dinner with crisp bacon on the top, or a melted cheese sandwich and for breakfast scrambled eggs covered with melted cheddar cheese and several pieces of crisp bacon and maybe a piece of toast. This is ALL she ever ate with her Pepsi, and Pepsi is all she ever drank. Her caregivers prepared mashed potato bowls into the frig so there were always meals ready when she wanted one. She was a gracious host, offering hugs, food, Pepsi, snacks and to open the window or go outside when she lit up a Pall Mall.

As the months turned into years, I witnessed her courage, facing her fear of the unknown, letting go to the unraveling, and the loss of her memoried-self. In the final years our weekend visits included her beloved care giver Lynn. The three of us became close friends and shared a deep love and profound spiritual connection.

Sally and I were owls. We stayed up into the wee hours of the morning. As her Alz-doula I sat at the table in the quiet holding her in loving light while she carried out various organizing tasks, I didn't need to understand. Sally talked with herself and asked questions. Sometimes we talked, mostly we didn't. I was her companion bearing witness to and holding space for her to integrate her profound loss. I'd begin to fade around 2 a.m. and go to bed. She'd be up for a couple more hours before she slept. In the morning Sally would be fresh and upbeat greeting my groggy self with a booming, "Good morning honey." In time Sally adjusted to her reality. She was lucid, loving, funny, focused, flirtatious, thoughtful, and kept her ability to listen closely and draw people to her. Sally was always Sally.

She believed in magic
Sally was magic
A light being
A loving spirit
Beginning and ending
With unconditional love
Sally embodied the spirit of aloha

During our precious time together, I collected her sage one liners.

These are but a few.

We are all molecules.
We are in relationship with all.
The essence of love is a force field.
Understanding is an act of consciousness.
I believe with god, to recognize god in all living things.

Magic mushrooms have their own playhouse.
If you haven't been told you live on Cloud 9
You haven't been doing your work.

♀ ♀ ♀

A time will come
Do I know you? Have we met before? You're so familiar.
We must have known each other In another life.
And we'll laugh and laugh
And be fast friends
Again

BOOK REVIEWS

Carnival Lights by **Christ Stark**
Modern History Press, October 2021
267 pages, $24.95

Reviewed by Judith Katz

Chris Stark's remarkable novel, *Carnival Lights*, is many things: On one level it is the story of two teenage Ojibwe cousins, Kristen and Sher as they run away to Minneapolis from their home on the Goodhue Reservation in the summer of 1969. Their aim is to get to the neon lights of the Minnesota State Fair. Kristen's aim is to escape her murderously abusive father. Sher is along as her guide and butch protector. While they hope for safety and adventure, like the heroes of every odyssey tale, the young women's journey is fraught with danger at every turn.

If the story of Kristen and Sher's trek away from their home on the reservation were all there was to *Carnival Lights*, that would be plenty. But Stark's tale is a kaleidoscopic one, framed cinematically in layers of magical realism and historical non-fiction, woven through with sagas of cultural and personal survival. As the young women make their way through the perils of Minneapolis street life (pimps, dealers, cops, political riots, drugs and predators), Stark inserts clear eyed history lessons, beginning in her prologue describing the village of Point Park Minnesota in August 1860.

> The carnival came to town, but not until after the Indian bones were excavated. Under the red beam of the Minnesota Point Lighthouse cast by a fourth-order Fresnel lens and illuminated by a kerosene lamp, a motley assortment of Finnish, German, and French men wielding spades and pick axes broke joints, cracked femurs, shattered fingers, and split the skulls of those buried long before Europeans set foot on the shores of the westernmost tip of Gitchi Gami, renamed Lake Superior by the French (Carnival Lights, i).

With every instance of violence and attempted violence against the Kristen and Sher, Stark has inserted a parallel example of its historical antecedent or an example of how shared traditional knowledge and memory gives the cousins the skills to survive.

When the cousins finally complete their journey, sleeping in deserted buildings, damp stairwells, under bridges and over passes, and get to the Minnesota State Fair, Stark shows us the grease coated, sweaty throngs, evokes the smells (delicious and putrid), and the garish lights and carnival sounds that are still, even in the 21st century, the Minnesota State Fair. Even at the fair—perhaps especially at the fair—all of Stark's elements come together as she relates in her clear sardonic voice the history of the land on which the fair has been built and the calculation involved in in deciding which attractions would be presented to draw in the most money from the fair going public.

The story of two of these attractions, in 1957, a V-2 Nazi rocket, "...displaying it at that year's fair on a plot of open land behind the oldest French fry stand at the fair, opened in 1932..." (*Carnival Lights*, pp 190) and a newer attraction, The Mexican Village:

> This was a change decreed by the State Agricultural Society during a meeting in February, 1968. At that

meeting, Ada Pritchard, a fourteen-year member of the State Agricultural Society and great-great-granddaughter of the first pastor of Westminster Presbyterian... stated, "...It's time the fair catches up to the progressive race ways of state and national politics... by creating a location designated specifically for our darker skinned brethren to display their crafts...And, I might add...people have come to enjoy their food..." *Carnival Lights* pp 195

Chris Stark does not shy away from relating every bit of abuse that reverberates through the story of the cousins, their families, and their culture—and at times, to be honest, it feels like a lot. But at this writing, as at least 16 states have introduced legislation preventing public educators from introducing and teaching ideas about the racist history of this country; any mention of words implying the normalcy of homosexuality; as the health and wellbeing of transgender children is being called into question as are our rights to choose vis Roe v. Wade; as books are being banned from schools and libraries because their subject matter is deemed uncomfortable and dangerous by some-- I can think of no more important time to read and buy Chris Stark's *Carnival Lights*.

CONTRIBUTORS

Jennifer Beach is a long-term prison abolitionist who lives and works in San Francisco. She teaches English composition at San Francisco State University and codirects Prison Radio because she is convinced that only by hearing underrepresented voices can we chart a future of positive social change. She is endlessly grateful to have been part of Out of Control and loves the many lesbians who help us chart a new idea of a liberated future.

Chrystos has been the recipient of the Sappho Award of Distinction from the Astraea Lesbian Foundation for Justice, NEA and Barbara Deming grants, and the Human Rights Freedom of Expression Award, in addition to winning the Audre Lorde International Poetry Competition. Chrystos's work as a poet and activist spans Native land and treaty rights; freedom for imprisoned Indigenous activists; and feminist, two-spirit, and lesbian solidarity. A proudly self-educated poet, Chrystos's powerful work celebrates sovereignty and desire as counterforces against colonialism, genocide, patriarchy, and hegemony. Chrystos taught writing inside FCI Dublin, California, and helped to organize and read her poetry at Out of Control's annual cultural event Sparks Fly. She is a resident of Ocean Shores, WA.

Through her activism and scholarship over many decades, **Angela Davis** has been deeply involved in movements for social justice around the world. Her work as an educator—both at the university level and in the larger public sphere—has always emphasized the importance of building communities of struggle for economic, racial, and gender justice.

Professor Davis's teaching career has taken her to San Francisco State University, Mills College, and UC Berkeley. She also has taught at UCLA, Vassar, Syracuse University, the Claremont

Colleges, and Stanford University. Most recently she spent fifteen years at the University of California, Santa Cruz, where she is now Distinguished Professor Emerita of History of Consciousness—an interdisciplinary PhD program—and of Feminist Studies.

Angela Davis is the author of ten books and has lectured throughout the United States as well as in Europe, Africa, Asia, Australia, and South America. In recent years a persistent theme of her work has been the range of social problems associated with incarceration and the generalized criminalization of those communities that are most affected by poverty and racial discrimination. She draws upon her own experiences in the early seventies as a person who spent eighteen months in jail and on trial, after being placed on the FBI's Ten Most Wanted list. She also has conducted extensive research on numerous issues related to race, gender, and imprisonment. Her books include *Abolition Democracy* and *Are Prisons Obsolete?*, as well as two books of essays entitled *The Meaning of Freedom* and *Freedom Is a Constant Struggle: Ferguson, Palestine, and the Foundations of a Movement*. Her most recent books include a reissue of *Angela Davis: An Autobiography* and *Abolition. Feminism. Now.*, with coauthors Gina Dent, Erica Meiners, and Beth Richie.

Angela Davis is a founding member of Critical Resistance, a national organization dedicated to the dismantling of the prison industrial complex. Internationally, she is affiliated with Sisters Inside, an abolitionist organization based in Queensland, Australia, that works in solidarity with women in prison.

Like many educators, Professor Davis is especially concerned with the general tendency to devote more resources and attention to the prison system than to educational institutions. Having helped to popularize the notion of a "prison industrial complex," she now urges her audiences to think seriously about the future possibility of a world without prisons and to help forge a twenty-first-century abolitionist movement.

In 2001, **Linda Evans** was released from prison after serving 16+ years as a political prisoner for actions against white supremacy and US imperialism. She cofounded All of Us or None, a national civil rights organization of formerly incarcerated people and their families. She is currently organizing with CCWP (California Coalition for Women Prisoners) and California's statewide DROP LWOP Coalition, fighting to eliminate life-without-parole sentences. Linda serves on several advisory boards and is active in the Immigrant Defense Taskforce of North Bay Organizing Project in Santa Rosa.

Noelle Hanrahan is a lesbian, journalist, private investigator, and lawyer. Noelle Hanrahan and Out of Control member Jennifer Beach founded Prison Radio and have been recording Mumia Abu-Jamal audio commentaries for thirty years. Noelle has been deeply inspired by the women of Out of Control and *UltraViolet*, who make revolution fun and possible. She now lives in Philadelphia.

Emily Hobson is a historian of radicalism, sexuality, and race in the United States, and an interdisciplinary scholar of queer studies, American Studies, and critical ethnic studies. Emily's research centers on radical and queer politics in the latter half of the twentieth century. She is the author of two books: *Lavender and Red: Liberation and Solidarity in the Gay and Lesbian Left*, and (with Dan Berger) *Remaking Radicalism: A Grassroots Documentary Reader of the United States, 1973–2001*. Her newest book project examines the history of HIV/AIDS activism by, for, and with imprisoned people in the 1980s and 1990s United States.

Brooke Lober is a teacher, writer, and social movement scholar who is currently researching legacies of antiracist and anti-Zionist feminisms in the Bay Area. Brooke's writing is published in the scholarly journals *Feminist Formations*; *Women's Studies*; *Journal of Lesbian Studies*; *Meridians: Feminism, Race, Transnationalism*; *Abolition: A Journal of Insurgent Politics*; and on numerous websites of radical culture. She is coeditor of *Abolition Feminisms*, two volumes of abolition feminist writing and art, forthcoming with Haymarket Press in 2022.

Gemma Mirkinson is a labor and delivery nurse and has been a radical in the Bay Area community for much of her life. She lives in San Francisco with her partner, daughter, and large extended family.

Judith Mirkinson (Mirk) is a longtime women's and human rights activist. A dedicated anti-imperialist and feminist, she has viewed solidarity with political prisoners as a core component of her politics. She has spent decades doing international solidarity work and is particularly interested in the relationship between gender violence and militarization. As such she has worked with women internationally from Afghanistan, Haiti, and the Philippines among others, and is a cofounder of San Francisco Women in Black. Most recently she is a coauthor of the 2019 National Lawyers Guild report "The Lasalin Massacre and the Human Rights Crisis in Haiti." She is the current president of the "Comfort Women" Justice Coalition.

Jay Mullins (she/her) belligerent activist, union electrician, cofounder of the first union shop owned and operated by women electricians in San Francisco, lives in Portland, Oregon, with her partner Chris, daughter Ruby, and cat Jackson.

Blue Murov is a lesbian, longtime activist, and amateur luthier who builds stringed instruments. She learned desktop publishing while working on *Out of Time*, and she designs the photo illustration for the front-page political satire articles in *UltraViolet*. She lives in Pacifica, CA.

Tanya Napier lives in the East Bay with her teenage daughter. She currently works for Kaiser Permanente as a receptionist. She loves spending her free time with her daughter.

Zulma Oliveras Vega is a Puerto Rican lesbian and a human rights activist who was born in San Germán, Puerto Rico. She is an advocate for the freedom of political prisoners, participated in protests in Chiapas & Vieques, and traveled to Palestine as part of the group International Solidarity Movement. While living in California, she served on the board of directors of Bay Area Boricuas, was a former member of Comité Por Un Puerto Rico Libre (Committee for a Free Puerto Rico), and cofounded MASA, Mujeres de ambiente: sociales y activas (Lesbian Women: Social and Active). She was also a member of the Sparks Fly Committee, and the San Francisco Dyke March. Zulma has organized many musical and cultural events, is published in several anthologies, and has her own poetry books. She is currently working at Coordinadora Paz Para la Mujer (Coalition Peace for Women) as the social empowerment specialist and supervises the Trans Task Force of Puerto Rico.

Dylcia Pagán is the daughter of Puerto Rican migrant parents, born in the Bronx and raised in El Barrio–East Harlem, New York City. She is an activist, teacher, former political prisoner, author, poet, visual artist, and healer. As a young activist, Dylcia worked for the Community Development Agency of the City of New York evaluating poverty programs, as the program director of Aguilar Senior Citizen Center in East Harlem, and as director of the youth summer program El Grito del Barrio. Dylcia was a member of the FALN, the Fuerzas Armadas de Liberación Nacional. While underground, she was arrested in 1980, charged with seditious conspiracy for fighting for the independence of Puerto Rico, and sentenced to sixty-three years of imprisonment. During her incarceration (1980–99), Pagán engaged in cultural and social activities, including directing a theater company, The Caged Bird Players; organizing a daycare center; and creating a holistic health program. Since her release, she has continued her work as an activist, media-maker, and artist. She lives in Puerto Rico.

Julie Perini makes experimental and documentary films/videos. She's the recipient of numerous grants, awards, and residencies and has exhibited her work internationally. Julie is an associate professor of art practice at Portland State University. She is a backcountry guide with the arts/environmental organization Signal Fire. Originally from the East Coast, she now lives in Portland, Oregon, among an inspiring community of artists and activists.

Frankie Free Ramos is from Yauco, Puerto Rico, spent much of her childhood in San Diego, and has lived in the Bay Area since moving to Berkeley for undergraduate studies in the early 1990s. After obtaining a teaching credential and masters in teaching from the University of San Francisco, Frankie worked for over ten years in various high school settings. She recently earned a PhD from the UC Berkeley Graduate School of Education in leadership, policy, and politics. Her scholarship and activism focus on community organizing and social movements toward educational justice and transformation, and what a decolonizing and abolitionist praxis demand in the current sociopolitical context. She has been a long-time activist for the decolonization of Puerto Rico, freedom for political prisoners, and an end to privatization and the politics of austerity in education. She currently serves as the director of campaigns and organizing at CURYJ (Communities United for Restorative Youth Justice), a community-based organization in Oakland, CA, working to end youth incarceration and unlock the leadership of young people to dream beyond bars. Frankie has three children with her partner, Bay Area legendary MC Rico Pabón. The family loves to enjoy the outdoors together and spread love in the world!

Kate Raphael is a radical feminist, queer activist, novelist, journalist, and office worker. She is a producer on KPFA radio's *Women's Magazine* and a member of the *UltraViolet* editorial collective. She most cherishes the letters *UltraViolet* receives from queer prisoners. Her Palestine mystery novels have won numerous independent book awards and been nominated for a Lambda Award. She now lives in Seattle.

Lucy Rodríguez Vélez and Alicia Rodríguez Vélez are former Puerto Rican political prisoners who spent almost twenty years in prison for defending the self-determination and decolonization of Puerto Rico.

Susan Rosenberg is a human rights and prisoners' rights advocate, adjunct lecturer, award-winning writer, speaker, and former prisoner. Her memoir, *An American Radical*, details her 16+ years in federal prison and her conclusions about her prison experience. She was released from prison in 2001 through executive clemency by then-president Bill Clinton. Susan has worked in nonprofit communications on human rights and in defense of prisoners and the abolition of prisons. She is a member of the Family and Friends of Dr. Mutulu Shakur and is involved in other political prisoner–release efforts. She is an adjunct lecturer at Hunter College in the women and gender studies department. She has been on the board of directors of Thousand Currents, an international development organization, and a former member of the board of Ladies of Hope Ministries, a women's and girls' reentry organization. She is on the board of advisors of Alliance for Families for Justice and a member of the PEN Prison Writing Committee at PEN America. She is a contributor to the upcoming revised edition of the *PEN America Handbook for Writers in Prison*. She lives in Brooklyn, New York, and continues to write.

Penny Schoner, political activist since the 1960s in the Bay Area, friend of Marilyn Buck and political prisoners across the country, is a paralegal who works with attorneys to free prisoners who have served time far beyond their court-ordered sentences. Out of Control brought Penny new depths of understanding the viciousness of discrimination and incarceration.

Jane Segal is a longtime social justice activist, lesbian mom, feminist, founding member of Out of Control, and coeditor of this issue of Sinister Wisdom. The focus of her adult activist life has been her commitment to advocating for women locked in cages, especially women political prisoners, and fighting for the abolition of the prison industrial complex. Jane was also a teacher, working and developing curricula in various settings. She especially enjoys hands-on, project-based learning. As the director of a girls' after-school program, she was one of the founders of the Alliance for Girls. She lives in San Francisco with her girlfriend.

Judy Siff is a longtime social justice activist. She is a former political prisoner, current psychotherapist, lesbian mother, artist, and ongoing tai chi student. She lives in SF with her partner of forty years and their dogs.

Julie Starobin is still a lesbian, still an activist, and still works on the radical queer newsletter *UltraViolet*. She lives with her girlfriend and their dog in Pacifica, CA.

Laura Whitehorn served 14+ years in federal prison for the "Resistance Conspiracy" case. Released in 1999, she cofounded Release Aging People in Prison/RAPP (RAPPCampaign.com), committed to ending the racist punishment system and freeing political prisoners. She edited *The War Before* by the late Safiya Bukhari, a Black Panther and political prisoner. Whitehorn helped organize the 2014 exhibit *Self-Determination Inside/Out* at Interference Archive in Brooklyn, showing how the struggles of incarcerated people shape social movements outside. She and her longtime partner Susie Day participated in a 2016 prison, labor, and academic delegation to Palestine.

Sinister Wisdom
A Multicultural Lesbian Literary & Art Journal

SUBSCRIBE TODAY!

Subscribe using the enclosed subscription card or online at
www.SinisterWisdom.org/subscribe using PayPal

Or send check or money order to
Sinister Wisdom - 2333 McIntosh Road, Dover, FL 33527-5980

Sinister Wisdom accepts gifts of all sizes to support the journal.

Sinister Wisdom is free on request to women in prisons and psychiatric institutions.

Back issues available!

Sinister Wisdom **Back Issues Available**

126 Out of Control ($14)
125 Glorious Defiance / Work by Disabled Lesbians ($14)
124 Deeply Held Beliefs ($14)
123 A Tribute to Conditions ($14)
122 Writing Communities ($14)
121 Eruptions of Inanna ($17.95)
114 A Generous Spirit ($18.95)
108 For The Hard Ones Para las duras ($18.95)
107 Black Lesbians—We Are the Revolution! ($14)
104 Lesbianima Rising: Lesbian-Feminist Arts in the South, 1974–96 ($12)
103 Celebrating the Michigan Womyn's Music Festival ($12)
102 The Complete Works of Pat Parker ($22.95) Special Limited edition hardcover ($35)
98 Landykes of the South ($12)
96 What Can I Ask ($18.95)
93 Southern Lesbian-Feminist Herstory 1968–94 ($12)
91 Living as a Lesbian ($17.95)
88 Crime Against Nature ($17.95)
80 Willing Up and Keeling Over
49 The Lesbian Body
48 Lesbian Resistance Including work by Dykes in Prison
47 Lesbians of Color: Tellin' It Like It 'Tis
46 Dyke Lives
43/44 15th Anniversary double-size (368 pgs) retrospective

- Sister Love: The Letters of Audre Lorde and Pat Parker ($14.95)
- Notes for a Revolution ($14)

Back issues are $6.00 unless noted plus $3.00 Shipping & Handling for 1st issue; $1.00 for each additional issue. Order online at www.sinisterwisdom.org

Or mail check or money order to:
Sinister Wisdom
2333 McIntosh Road
Dover, FL 33527-5980